Excel

BASIC SKILLS

ENGLISH

YEAR 6

AGES 11–12

ENGLISH WORKBOOK

Get the Results You Want!

PASCAL PRESS

Kristine Brown

Reprinted 2006, 2008, 2009, 2010 (twice), 2012, 2013, 2017, 2018, 2020, 2022

ISBN 978 1 74125 159 3

Pascal Press
PO Box 250
Glebe NSW 2037
(02) 8585 4050
www.pascalpress.com.au

Publisher: Vivienne Joannou
Series developer: Kristine Brown
Project editor: Emma Driver
Edited by Christine Eslick
Page design and layout by Jelly Design
Typesetting by Alena Jencik, Grand Graphix Pty Ltd
Cover by DiZign Pty Ltd
Photos by Digital Vision, Photos.com
Printed by Vivar Printing/Green Giant Press

Contents

Acknowledgements

I would like to thank the following students, authors, publishers and organisations for their very kind permission to use their writing in this book:

William McLean, for his recount "Scott of the Antarctic" page 2
Allen & Unwin, for the cover of *Lionheart* on page 8
Hannah Kirby, for her story "Survivor" page 10 (Hannah's story was a Queensland regional winner in the 2004 Nestlé Write Around Australia Competition)
Scholastic Australia Pty Ltd, for the writing tip by Morris Gleitzman on page 15 (from Eyespy Magazine, no. 5, 1993. Text copyright Scholastic Australia, 1993. First published by Scholastic Australia Pty Ltd, 1993.)
Elizabeth Honey and Allen & Unwin, for the poems "I lie straight", "Drifting off" and "My bike" and the illustration (from *Mongrel Doggerel*) on page 18
Chris Davies and Stephen Pitt, for their procedural recount "Bridge Building" on page 29
Mercia Hamilton and Erin Wilson Leary, for their procedural recount "Building Towers" on page 30
Joe Brown, for his letter on page 34
Joy Tarasenko, for her letter on page 38, and the *Blue Mountains Gazette*
Libby Gleeson and Scholastic Australia Pty Ltd, for the extract from *My Story: The Rum Rebellion: The Diary of David Bellamy* on page 50
Maria Masri, for her speech "Zoos are cruel places. Do you agree?" on page 58
Patrick Thomas, for his explanation "What causes a tsunami?" on page 66
Kenny Chew, for his explanation "What causes an earthquake?" on page 66
The Department of Conservation, New Zealand, for the glacier texts on page 70

I would also like to thank Val Noake at the State Library of New South Wales and the Nestlé Write Around Australia for their help and cooperation in relation to the use of Hannah Kirby's story. Nestlé Write Around Australia is a Nestlé Good Life Program coordinated by the State Library of New South Wales and supported by state and public libraries around Australia.

My special thanks to the following teachers for advice and help with finding texts and for ideas on various aspects of the book:

Graeme Wilson, Julie Tomlins, Milly Kennedy, Jenny Williamson and Anne Wharton from Springwood Public School
Bill Guilfoyle from Ellison Public School
Lyn Maloney from James Erskine Public School
Debbie Jay from Arndell Anglican College
Rhonda Bassett from Bowning Public School.

Finally, my thanks go to the independent reviewers of the book for their thorough and constructive comments.

To the student

This book will help you with the writing you do every day at school—in English and in other subjects. Each chapter looks at a different type of writing. Some are imaginative text types such as narratives and poems. Others are factual text types—reports and explanations, for example.

All the chapters begin with a sample text. Make sure you read the sample text carefully and look at the special features marked on it.

You should then try the activities that follow. These give you guidance and practice in writing a similar type of text. Some activities help you with grammar and punctuation. Others focus on words—the way they are spelt and what they mean. Some activities are just for fun. Each chapter ends with activities to help you write a complete text yourself.

There are spaces in the workbook where you can write, but you will need your own paper for some of the writing activities at the end of the chapters. I suggest you buy a book or folder to put this writing in—let's call it your **Writer's Notebook**. If you like, you could use your Writer's Notebook for all the longer pieces of writing you do. It would also be a good place to put the bits and pieces you collect to give you ideas for writing —illustrations, advertisements, photographs, research information and so on.

Always have a dictionary nearby as you work through the chapters, and be sure to ask for help if you need it.

It is best to work through the book from Chapter 1 to the end, because in this way you will build on skills from one chapter to the next. However, you could also use the chapters as you need them. For example, you could do Chapter 10, "Writing a discussion", when you are doing this kind of writing at school.

Many of the sample texts throughout the book have been written by students of your own age. I really hope you enjoy reading them and then writing your own.

Have fun and good luck!

Kristine Brown

Chapter 1 Writing a factual recount

A factual recount gives the details about an event or events that actually happened, in the order that they happened. This factual recount is about historical events.

STRUCTURE

LANGUAGE

Scott of the Antarctic (1868–1912)

1. In the early 20th century, many people were interested in exploring the Antarctic. One of these was Robert Falcon Scott, a captain in the British Navy. Scott had already led one expedition to the region, but his ambition was to be the first person to actually reach the South Pole.

2. In 1910, Scott set out on his second expedition. The story of this expedition is one of the most tragic in the history of exploration. The expedition became a race when Scott found out during his journey that Roald Amundsen, a young Norwegian explorer, was already on his way to the Pole, better equipped and well ahead of him.

3. Scott's journey from this point on was filled with obstacles and hardship. For example, the Siberian ponies Scott had brought with him had to be shot because they were not suited for the long journey and got stuck in the deep snow. This resulted in the men having to pull the sledges during the hardest part of the journey. They were also caught in a ferocious blizzard—quite unexpected for that time of the year.

4. When the exhausted team finally arrived at the South Pole, they were bitterly disappointed to discover that the Norwegian flag was already flying high. They were a month too late. Fatigued and dejected, the team then had to turn around and start their 1300 kilometre trip back. On the way, the rations slowly ran out and the men got weaker and weaker. They were sick with frostbite and scurvy and they all thought they would perish.

5. One of the team members, Lawrence Oates, was in great pain and had gangrene. He knew he was slowing the team down, so one night he made an excuse to go outside the tent in a raging blizzard. He never came back.

6. Three weeks later, Scott and his men died in their little green tent. They were only 17 kilometres from their depot and from supplies that would have saved them.

7. Scott's last diary entry shows his courage and devotion to his men: "Every day now we have been ready to start for our depot 11 miles away, but outside the door of the tent it remains a scene of whirling drift. I do not think we can hope for any better things now. We shall stick it out to the end, but we are getting weaker of course. It seems a pity but I do not think I can write more. For God's sake, look after our people."

8. Robert Falcon Scott was truly an Antarctic hero.

William McLean

Orientation to topic—who, when, where

Series of events—told in order they occurred (chronological order)

Paragraphs organised by time periods

Comments on events

Conclusion rounds off recount and comments on events or people

Proper nouns to name individual people and places

Pronouns to refer back to people and things

Past tense verbs

Time words and phrases to show order of events

Interesting detail about events, people and places

What did you read?

1. Answer these questions.

   a How many times did Scott go to Antarctica? ____________________

   b Who was Scott racing to the South Pole? ____________________

   c How did Scott know that he had lost the race? ____________________

2. The Siberian ponies were a ____________________ (good? bad?) idea because ____________________

   ____

3. ***Fatigued*** and ***dejected*** (paragraph 4) are difficult words but you can work out their meanings from the words around them. Find another word in paragraph 4 that is close in meaning to:

   a fatigued ____________________

   b dejected ____________________

4. Underline the words in paragraph 4 that tell you the men would have been very hungry.

5. Do you think that Scott knew he and his men were going to die? (Give your reasons.) ____________________

   ____

How was it written?

1. The first paragraph of a recount usually gives the reader information that **orients** them to who or what the text is about. Tick the information mentioned in this first paragraph.

   Who it is about ____

   When the person was born ____

   What job or position the person had ____

   What the person had done before ____

   What the person wanted to do ____

   What his family thought about his goal ____

   The period in which the events happened ____

   Where the events took place ____

2. A recount should make it clear **when** and **in which order** things happened. Expressions such as ***then***, ***finally***, ***in 1910*** help do this. Find these sentences in the recount and underline the words that tell you about time and order.

   a … many people were interested in exploring the Antarctic. (paragraph 1)

   b … Scott set out on his second expedition. (paragraph 2)

   c Scott's journey … was filled with obstacles and hardships. (paragraph 3)

   d … , Scott and his men died in their little green tent. (paragraph 6)

3. Most factual recounts include details about people or events to make them interesting. Which details about Scott, his men and their expedition especially interested or affected you?

   ____

   ____

4. Why do you think William included Scott's last diary entry before his one-line conclusion?

   ____

   ____

Spelling and meaning

expedition	ambition	tragic	exploration	blizzard
obstacles	hardship	exhausted	disappointed	fatigued
dejected	rations	perish	courage	devotion

Tip for sensational spellers

A good way to learn new spellings is the **look–say–cover–write–check** method:
Look hard at the word, especially the difficult parts.
Say it out loud. Close your eyes and picture it in your mind while you say it.
Cover it up.
Write it without looking back.
Check it. If you get it right, write it once more.
If you get it wrong, do the **look–say–cover–write–check** method again till you get it right.

1 Try out the **look–say–cover–write–check** method with five words from the word box that you think look difficult. Use the lines below.

________________ ________________ ________________
________________ ________________ ________________
________________ ________________ ________________
________________ ________________ ________________
________________ ________________ ________________

Did it work? (yes? no? for some words only?) ____________________

2 Many of the words in the list end in ***-tion*** to make the sound "-shen". Which ***-tion*** word means:

a travelling around an unknown region? ________________

b an organised trip to achieve or discover something? ________________

c a goal in life? ________________

d care and attention? ________________

3 Choose words from the word box to complete these sentences.

a All explorers must have great ________________ to face the unknown.

b "________________" is a word meaning conditions that are hard for humans to bear.

c Without good planning, Antarctic explorers could ________________ in the snow and ice.

d The men faced the driving snow and intense cold of the worst ________________ on record.

e An exploration can easily fail if there are not enough ________________ to keep the team alive.

f The weather was just one of the many ________________ that Scott's team faced.

4 Here are some words you might use to describe explorers and their achievements. Can you fill in the missing letters?

a COU ___ A ___ EOU ___

b ___ ER ___ IC

c AD ___ EN ___ UROU ___

d DETER ___ ___ ___ ED

e E ___ TRA ___ RD ___ ___ AR ___

f B ___ L ___

g EX ___ ERIE ___ C ___ ___

h BRI ___ ___ IAN ___

i ___ AL ___ ANT

j D ___ RING

Grammar—Types of nouns

Let's look at what you know about nouns and types of nouns.
Nouns are words that **name** people, places, things and ideas in our world. Examples are ***explorers***, ***Scott***, ***officer***, ***ambition***.
We can divide nouns into common nouns and proper nouns. **Common nouns** name general kinds of people, places, things and ideas (e.g. ***ponies***, ***photo***, ***month***, ***frostbite***). **Proper nouns** name particular people, places or things (e.g. ***Antarctica***, ***Robert Falcon Scott***, ***South Pole***). Proper nouns always begin with capital letters.
We can also divide nouns into concrete and abstract nouns. **Concrete nouns** name things we can see or touch (e.g. ***flag***, ***explorer***, ***blizzard***). **Abstract nouns** name ideas and feelings—things we cannot see or touch. Examples are ***ambition***, ***history***, ***hardship*** and ***discovery***.
In factual recounts we often need proper nouns to write about people, places and events.

The factual recount below is about Amelia Earhart, a very famous aviator. However, some nouns are missing. Can you put the nouns in the box back in the right place? [ ] means a proper noun is missing, ________ means a common noun is missing and ========= means an abstract noun is missing.

history	United States of America	trouble	Paris	plane	Earhart	years	storm
Equator	Wright brothers	flight	goal	pioneer			

Amelia Earhart was born in Kansas in the [ ] in 1898. She was just five ________ old when Orville and Wilbur Wright made their famous ________ at Kitty Hawk in North Carolina. Little did she know then that she would be just as famous in the ========= of aviation as the [ ].

In 1932, [ ] flew out of New Brunswick on the east coast of Canada aiming for Paris. She wanted to be the first person to successfully make a flight across the Atlantic Ocean. Unfortunately, a severe ________ forced her to land in Ireland, rather than [ ], but she had still achieved her =========. Sadly, she was dead only five years later, as she attempted to be the first person to circumnavigate the world. She struck ========= over the Pacific Ocean, just east of the International Dateline, and disappeared.

Thirty years later, the search for her ________ was renewed. On a small island just south of the [ ], a navigator's bookcase and part of a woman's shoe were found. It seems likely they belonged to this very brave aviation ________.

Punctuation—Commas and colons

We use **commas** for many different reasons. In these sentences, the comma **separates a phrase** that adds detail to the main idea (e.g. about who, when, where, how, or why).

Examples In 1910, he set out on his second expedition.

Fatigued and dejected, the team then had to turn around and start their 1300 kilometre trip back.

One of the team members, Lawrence Oates, was in great pain and had gangrene.

1 Add commas to these sentences where they are needed to separate phrases.

- **a** As a young boy Ernest Shackleton longed for adventure and excitement.
- **b** Despite all the hardships they were determined to continue their voyage.
- **c** After a slow journey through pack ice their ship finally reached its destination.
- **d** In 1778 Captain James Cook was the most famous explorer of his time.
- **e** In 1871 David Livingstone the greatest African explorer of all time had been missing for six years.
- **f** The *New York Herald* sent Henry Stanley an experienced reporter to find Livingstone.

Colons (**:**) are often used to introduce **a quotation**.

Example Scott's last diary entry shows his courage and his devotion to his men: "Every day now we have …"

Colons are also often used to introduce **a list of items**.

Example They needed three things: good weather, good equipment and good luck.

Reminders

- You need quotation marks to show the actual words quoted.
- You need commas to separate the items in a list.

2 Add colons, commas and quotation marks to these sentences where needed.

- **a** There were four dogs Henry Jacky Nino and Nina.
- **b** He wrote I can't go on any further.
- **c** The trip has three stages sailing there climbing the mountains and setting up camp.
- **d** Remember these things travel in a group let someone know your route and take a safety kit.
- **e** His first words were Welcome to you all.

Can you help?

These paragraphs are from a recount of the expedition across Australia from south to north by Robert O'Hara Burke and William Wills. However, they are in the wrong order. Can you sort them out? Use the time expressions in *italics* to help you. (The first paragraph is already done.)

a _1_ On 16 December, Burke and Wills, set out towards the north coast with two other men, Charles Gray and John King. They left William Brahe with four men, at a place called Coopers Creek, to wait for them to return.

b ___ *After a short rest*, the three men set off again, but they left a note in case Brahe came back. Brahe did come back, but sadly he did not see Burke's note. He rode away not knowing that his friends were near death only a few kilometres away.

c ___ *At first*, the small party made good progress. However, near the north coast of Australia it became extremely difficult. The land was like a jungle and it rained non-stop. Soon it was impossible to go on.

d ___ *Only days from their goal*, the four men had to turn around and begin the long journey back to Coopers Creek—over 1000 kilometres away. The rains kept falling and the four men became ill. Supplies were very low. On 17 April, Charles Gray, the strongest of them all, died.

e ___ *Within days*, Burke and Wills were both dead. Sadly, Wills died alone but King was with Burke till the end. Burke's last words to King were: "I hope you will remain with me here till I am quite dead. It is a comfort to know that someone is by." After three months, a rescue party found King barely alive, despite the care given to him by the local Aborigines.

f ___ *The next year*, Australia was crossed from south to north by John McDougall Stuart. Although Stuart won the prize, Burke and Wills were honoured for really being the first to cross the continent.

g ___ *Four days later*, the three weak and hungry survivors crawled into their camp at Coopers Creek. The camp was deserted. Brahe had left it that very morning—only eight hours before! Imagine their disappointment.

Puzzle time

Can you complete this crossword about explorers and exploration?

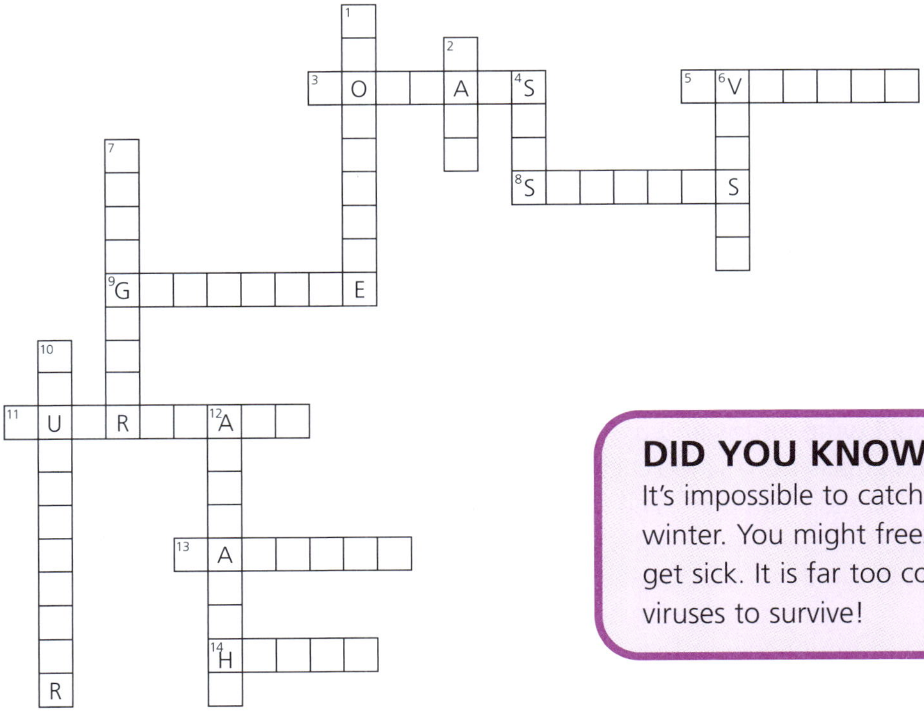

DID YOU KNOW?

It's impossible to catch a cold in the Antarctic in winter. You might freeze to death, but you won't get sick. It is far too cold for most bacteria and viruses to survive!

Across:

3. Any explorer would be lost without this important item.
5. Another word for 'pilot'
8. For carrying luggage across ice (Santa uses these to carry presents!)
9. This terrible disease is an infection that can follow 1 Down.
11. A huge wind that can cause great damage on land or at sea
13. Many ships travelling in polar regions get stuck in this.
14. A kind of dog often used in ice and snow

Down:

1. This is a huge problem for polar explorers. It can cause fingers and toes to fall off.
2. This simple kind of sailing vessel has been used to cross vast oceans.
4. ________ are now used mostly for fun sports but polar explorers really needed them.
6. This is a general word for a boat or ship.
7. The person in an expedition whose job is to find the way.
10. A person who climbs mountains. Sir Edmund Hillary was one of these.
12. A huge fall of ice and snow. Very dangerous!

Your turn to write

Tips for extra-extraordinary writers

It is important to get your facts in the right order *before* you start writing a factual recount.
Use time expressions to help your reader follow the order of events (but try to think of other expressions besides ***then*** and ***next***).

1 You might have heard about Jesse Martin. Jesse is a modern-day explorer—but a very, very young one! Jesse was only 17 years old when he set off on his own to sail around the world.

Use the notes below to write a short recount about Jesse. (You don't have to use every fact.)

- Australian, German-born
- In 1999 became the youngest person to sail single-handed, non-stop around the world
- At 13 years old read about Thor Heyerdahl who sailed the oceans in a raft, the *Kon-Tiki*
- Began to plan a trip around the world—non-stop, alone and unassisted
- Knew how to sail but no experience on open seas
- Found people to teach him navigation and survival skills
- 6 December 1998—17 years old—sailed out of Melbourne's Port Phillip Bay
- 600 people waved him off. Boat called *Lionheart*; 10.23 metres long
- Enough food for 9 months and water for one cup a day
- Boat—solar powered—could write emails and use telephone
- Did school work, answered emails from schoolchildren, played guitar
- Worst part was terrible loneliness—sometimes cried
- Many storms. Worst storm—Cape of Good Hope, South Africa
- 328 days—sailed into Port Phillip Bay 31 October 1999—25 000 people greeted him
- Wrote a book—*Lionheart: A Journey of the Human Spirit*
- Wants to encourage other young people to follow their dreams and believe in themselves

Jesse Martin's book about his around-the-world journey, published in 2000.

These time expressions might help you to link some of the events: from then on, since then, during that time, during those years, meanwhile, this time, while at sea.

Orientation (Who? When? Where?) ____

____

____

____

____

____

____

Events (What happened before the journey? During the journey? At the end of the journey?)

____

____

____

Conclusion and comment (What do you think of Jesse?)

2. Is there an explorer you are especially interested in? See what you can find out about him or her from books or the Internet, and then write a recount about his or her life or expeditions. You will need to use your own paper—look back at the suggestion to buy a Writer's Notebook on page 1. Remember:
   - Write an orientation to the people, places and events.
   - Write the events in the order that they happened.
   - Add your own comments on the events (e.g. how the explorers must have felt).
   - Give interesting details.
   - Use time expressions to link the events, and write in the past tense.
   - Write a conclusion, including your own comment on the explorer.
   - Proofread your recount for spelling, punctuation and grammar.

Answers on pages 90–91

Chapter 2 Writing a narrative

In a narrative, your aim is to tell a story about events in a way that interests and entertains the reader.

STRUCTURE

Orientation (who, what, where and when)

Complication—unusual event or events that add interest and tension to the story

Short paragraphs (even one line) to help build interest and tension

Climax—the highest point of excitement or tension in the story

Resolution the complication is resolved in some way

Comment (or **coda**) on events (e.g. a lesson to be learnt)

Survivor

1. The hairs prickled on the back of my neck and a knot grew in the pit of my stomach at the sound of the gravel on the driveway and the thundering steps of Aunt Bessie, as she climbed the front stairs. The idea of a **terrifying death sliced through my heart like a cold, sharp blade**. What responsible parents would leave their daughter with a possible killer?!!

2. Aunt Mary, Uncle Marty and Grandpa all died in Aunt Bessie's care. Mum said one had an accident, one a crippling disease and Grandpa of old age … but **I** wasn't going to take any chances!

3. I knew I was going to have to be alert to survive the night.

4. The door flew open and a cold gust of wind rattled through the house. A definite sign! How were Mum and Dad oblivious to it?

5. Her first attempt on my life was barely seconds into the visit as her large arms grasped me, nearly cutting off my air supply. I looked at my parents with desperation, but did they help? No! They just smiled and left.

6. Aunt Bessie cleverly brought dinner with her but it was no ordinary dinner. It contained mountains of awful, overcooked veggies that were hardly warm and a three day old stew with lumpy gravy. **She** said it was to save Mum from cooking, but it was obviously the second attempt on my life.

7. The danger mounted as she began serving …

8. What would Charlie's Angels do in a situation like this?

9. I had to **think** quickly … I **slipped** into the shadows of the lounge room and quickly made a phone call to my friend, Jo.

10. "Please ring here in a few minutes and keep the babysitter on the phone for as long as possible. My life depends on it. I'll explain later. Thanks."

11. I tried to avoid taking a mouthful for as long as I could. Then, thank goodness, the phone rang, and as Aunt Bessie went to answer it, I wasted no time disposing of the poisonous meal before she returned.

12. **A narrow escape.**

13. Just as I thought the night could not get any worse, Aunt Bessie announced, with an evil grin, that it was time for bed and that she had a special bedtime story to read to me.

14. A bedtime story? Horror of horrors!

15. No amount of explaining could make her understand that twelve year olds do not go to bed at 7.30 and that I could read by myself.

16. Her failed attempts on my life had now led her to resort to death by slow torture.

17. I squirmed painfully in bed as she read her favourite bedtime story "Famous Five Go Camping" in a slow, boring voice.

18. When I thought I could endure no more and almost welcomed death, I heard the sound of the gravel on the driveway and the clatter of my Mum's high heels on the front stairs and knew … **I was a survivor**.

Hannah Kirby

LANGUAGE

Opening instantly gets reader's interest

Descriptive language

First person narration (but many stories are narrated in third person—*he*, *she*)

Pronouns to refer back to people (e.g. *she* refers to *Aunt Bessie*)

Narrator questions herself to show thoughts and feelings

Action verbs

Feeling and thinking verbs

Dialogue to make story lively

Phrases for dramatic effect

Past tense

What did you read?

1. Why does the narrator (the character telling the story) think that her Aunt Bessie might be dangerous? ______________________________

2. What is the cold gust of wind (paragraph 4) a sign of? ______________________________

3. Circle the best answer. In the narrator's opinion, how did Aunt Bessie first try to kill her?
   a By poisoning her   b By torturing her   c By suffocating her

4. Why does the narrator ring her friend Jo? ______________________________

   ____

5. What is described as slow torture? ______________________________

6. Circle the best answer. How do you think the narrator *really* feels towards Aunt Bessie?
   a She is terrified that Aunt Bessie will try to kill her.
   b She is terrified that Aunt Bessie will accidentally kill her.
   c She really hates having Aunt Bessie babysit her.

7. You could say that Hannah called her story "Survivor" because her main character survived her Aunt Bessie's attempts on her life. But I think Hannah means something else too—something we all have to survive as part of a family: OUR R ___ L ___ T ___ VES! What do you think?

How was it written?

1. Hannah captures our interest in the first paragraph of "Survivor". How does she do this? Tick the statements below you agree with.
   a She describes the narrator's feelings very vividly. ____
   b She makes us curious about Aunt Bessie. ____
   c She makes us wonder what might happen next. ____

2. Many narratives have a series of events that make up the complication. "Survivor" has three events. What are they?

   First event ______________________________

   Second event ______________________________

   Third event ______________________________

3. Hannah uses some very expressive words and phrases to describe what happens. What word does she use instead of these more common ones?

   a loud (para. 1) ____________   b cut (para. 1) ____________

   c blew (para. 4) ____________   d grabbed (para. 5) ____________

   e grew (para. 7) ____________   f went (para. 9) ____________

4. Hannah finds ways to tell us her thoughts and feelings without saying "I thought" or "I felt" all the time. Look back at the text and underline the words she uses instead of saying these things:
   a I thought I would die. (orientation)   b I felt this was a sign of things to come. (complication)
   c I thought about what I could do to save myself. (complication)
   d I hate Aunt Bessie reading to me. (complication)

5. Hannah has written about experiences that are familiar to many children in an amusing way. Which of her experiences were familiar to you? (Did they make you laugh?) ______________________________

   ____

Spelling and meaning

stomach	responsible	accident	crippling	disease
alert	rattled	definite	oblivious	obviously
situation	poisonous	announced	attempts	squirmed

Tip for snappy spellers
When you can't remember how to spell a word, write it out a few different ways to see which way **looks** right. Often you will quickly recognise the correct spelling. For example, when trying to write ***accident*** you might try
acksident ✗ acident ✗ accident ✓

1 Learn all the words from the word box using the **look–say–cover–write–check** method. (Remember the tip on p. 4.) Then choose one word to use in each space below.

a Marko ______________________ as his aunt tried to plant a big wet kiss on each cheek.

b The whole ________________ was my own fault so I felt totally ________________.

c Jana stayed wide awake and _________________________ throughout the night.

d We gasped in disbelief as Aunt Billa ___________________ that she would never return.

e My big brother, Rahul, was _________________________ to my discomfort.

f It was ________________ an ________________, but we still felt guilty.

g The pain was ________________ but somehow I had to go on.

h My ____________________ turned as I forced the revolting food down my throat.

Hannah describes her fear and anxiety by saying: *The hairs prickled on the back of my neck and a knot grew in the pit of my stomach.*
These kinds of expressions are called **idioms**. The words in idioms don't mean *exactly* what they say —the hairs don't really 'prickle' and there is not really a 'knot' in your stomach.

2 Which body part is missing from these idioms?

a My ____________________ went from under me. (terror)

b My ____________________ was in my mouth. (frightened)

c I felt weak at the ____________________. (great fear or great joy)

d He made my ____________________ boil. (anger)

e We were at each others' ____________________. (fighting)

f She couldn't keep a straight ____________________. (humour)

g Steam was coming out of my ____________________. (anger)

Grammar—Sentence review

Let's review what you know about sentences.
A **sentence** is a group of words that makes sense by itself. It contains a **subject and a verb**.
The subject is what the sentence is about—usually a noun (e.g. ***children***, ***dinner***). The verb is the doing, saying, thinking, being or having word.

A **simple sentence** has one message only (**one clause**).
Examples Hannah (subject) wrote (verb) a great story.
Aunt Mary, Uncle Marty and Grandpa all (subject) died (verb) in Aunt Bessie's care.

A **compound sentence** combines two (or more) clauses that are equally important and make sense by themselves (**independent clauses**). They are joined with ***and***, ***but*** or ***or***. In these examples the independent clauses are underlined.
Examples <u>The door flew open</u> and <u>a cold gust of wind rattled through the house</u>.
<u>Aunt Bessie cleverly brought dinner with her</u> but <u>it was no ordinary dinner</u>.

A **complex sentence** combines two (or more) clauses: one **main or independent clause** and one or more **supporting or dependent clauses**. In these examples the main clause is in **bold** and the dependent clause is <u>underlined</u>.
Examples **The danger mounted** <u>as she began serving</u>.
It contained mountains of overcooked veggies <u>that were hardly warm</u>.

1. Look at these simple sentences. Circle the subjects and underline the verbs.
   - a Bianca babysits her little sister, Yoli, every afternoon.
   - b My Uncle Ernie always rings up during our favourite telly program.
   - c You can watch the nature documentary.
   - d He talks for a very long time.
   - e Sometimes she is very naughty.
   - f Sasha and Julia stay with their cousins in the country every Christmas.
   - g You can go to bed right now.
   - h Their cousins never come to visit them in the city.

2. Look back at the simple sentences in activity 1 above. Can you join some up with ***and***, ***but*** or ***or*** to make compound sentences? Write your sentences out in the space below. One is done for you.

   Bianca babysits her little sister, Yoli, every afternoon, but sometimes she is very naughty.

   ____

   ____

   ____

   ____

3. Make complex sentences by drawing lines between the main (independent) clauses on the left and the dependent clauses on the right.

a My Aunty Dora makes soup	when my Uncle Vinnie gives me his famous bear hugs.
b I can hardly breathe	because she tells funny stories.
c I love my great grandmother	that smells like rotten fish.
d My cousins and I end up fighting	before we visit our Aunty Zita.
e Mum always gives us a lecture about being polite	every time we get together.

Punctuation—Question marks and exclamation marks

Question marks and **exclamation marks** can make your narrative **more interesting**. Look at these examples from Hannah's story:

What responsible parents would leave their daughter with a possible killer?!!

A bedtime story? Horror of horrors!

Warning: Don't use exclamation marks too much in a story or they will lose their impact.

Look at this extract from "Survivor". All the punctuation has been left out. Can you put it back? Check your work by looking back at the original.

aunt mary uncle marty and grandpa all died in aunt bessie's care mum said one had an accident one a crippling disease and grandpa of old age … but I wasn't going to take any chances

I knew I was going to have to be alert to survive the night

the door flew open and a cold gust of wind rattled through the house a definite sign how were mum and dad oblivious to it

her first attempt on my life was barely seconds into the visit as her large arms grasped me nearly cutting off my air supply I looked at my parents with desperation but did they help no they just smiled and left

Can you help?

It is important to give your readers some details to make your narrative 'come alive' for them. Can you add some detail to the beginning of this student's story to make it more interesting?

It was Wednesday. I was walking home with my brother up the hill that led to our house. It was hot. It was so hot. I hated this part of the walk home. I was scared of seeing the Nolan brothers outside their house. The Nolan brothers were very scary. Their house was scary too.

Close your eyes and try to imagine the scene, the writer's feelings and the atmosphere. What detail could you add, for example, about the day of the week and the time? your brother? the hill? the heat? the Nolan brothers? the Nolan brothers' house?

Write your version of the paragraph here. Add single words, phrases or whole sentences, and change some words if you want to.

Puzzle time

Can you match these famous characters to the books they appear in?

The Artful Dodger	*Winnie the Pooh*
Christopher Robin	*Matilda*
Erica Yurken	*The Wizard of Oz*
Peter, Susan, Edmund and Lucy	*The Magic Pudding*
Dorothy	*Hating Alison Ashley*
The Oompa Loompas	*Wind in the Willows*
The Lost Boys	*The Lion, the Witch and the Wardrobe*
Captain Haddock	*Oliver Twist*
Bunyip Bluegum	*Charlie and the Chocolate Factory*
The Mad Hatter	*Peter Pan and Wendy*
Mole, Rat, Badger and Toad	*Tintin*
Miss Trunchbull	*Alice's Adventures in Wonderland*

Your turn to write

Tip for totally tremendous writers

Check out this tip from a great story writer, Morris Gleitzman:

"Write about things that are important to you, and write about them using the sort of language you would normally use if you were just telling a friend about it. It's much better to use short words rather than long ones, common words rather than unusual ones. What makes you a writer is feeling passionately about something—hating it, loving it, finding it funny—and being able to put it on paper in a way that makes people who read it feel the same thing."

1. As Morris Gleitzman says, it's best to write about things that you feel strongly about, such as the things you hate, love or find funny. Let's try that now.

   Think about your daily life at home and school. Jot down two or three things you feel strongly about under the headings below. They might be situations, people (the way they look, the things they say), feelings, times of the day, school subjects or household chores.

   Hannah would have written down "Aunt Bessie babysitting" under "Things I hate".

Things I hate	**Things I love**	**Things I find funny**

2. Look through your lists and choose one topic that has potential for a story idea. Ask yourself: What are some of the especially interesting, exciting, funny or sad things about this topic? Now jot down some ideas. Hannah might have written under "Aunt Bessie babystitting":

very large	*can't breathe when she hugs me*	
cooking is terrible	*awful perfume*	*funny clothes*
mum and dad love her	*reads me baby books*	

3. Think about a complication for your topic—something unusual about the characters or events. (This is sometimes called the "What if" idea.) Ask yourself:
   - Is there another way to think about these people or events?
   - What could happen that is unusual, interesting, funny, sad?

   Now jot down a few possible complications for your topic. For example, Hannah thought "What if Aunt Bessie is actually trying to kill me".

4. Now you are ready to plan your narrative. Think about these questions:
   - How will you set up the story (the **orientation**)?
   - What is the **complication** (the "What if" idea)? How will you introduce it?
   - What will happen because of the first complication?
   - Will there be a high point of excitement and tension (**climax**) in your story?
   - How will your resolve your narrative (**resolution**)? Will it be funny? sad? serious? realistic? fantasy?
   - Will you add a comment on the events (**coda**)?

5. Draft your story on the next page. Use dialogue, interesting words and detail to make your story come alive. Check your spelling, punctuation and grammar, and then write your story out again in your Writer's Notebook (see suggestion, page 1).

Chapter 3 Writing a poem

Poems aim to express ideas and feelings about human experiences. Poems are usually meant to be read out loud, so the sound of the language is important. (Be sure to read these poems out loud before doing the activities.)

STRUCTURE

Interesting titles

Poems come in **many shapes and forms**—these do not have a regular rhythm (beat) or line length

Many poems use ***rhyme*** but these poems do not

Final lines usually round off ideas

I lie straight

I lie straight
eyes shut
Mum makes the bed
a soft silk breeze brushes me
as the sheet floats down
and settles on me
like a whisper

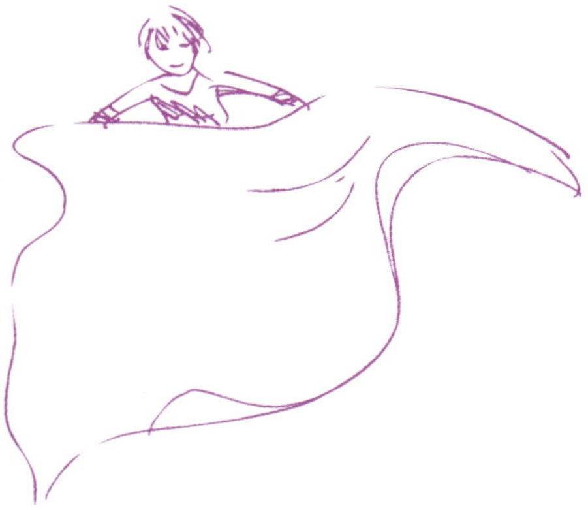

Drifting off

Hot summer nights I search for the cool patch.
Cold winter nights, curled up like a fox,
I hear the cars hiss on the road in the rain.
Sometimes I sing in my head while I'm waiting,
or pile on the blankets, to cook up dreams.
Just before I go to sleep, nothing hurts.
All the bumps and bruises
and my stiff legs are quiet.
I drift like a boat
Gently caught by the tide.

My bike

Dusk
wind whistles in my ears
smooth path
tyres hum
swooping through the gardens
no hands
sending the possums jumping for the trees
tailwind
I'm flying!

Poems and drawing from *Mongrel Doggerel* by Elizabeth Honey, Allen & Unwin, 1998. Printed with permission

LANGUAGE

Verbs create clear images of movements, sounds

Interesting details about experiences

***Comparing one thing to another* (similes)**

Alliteration—repetition of consonant sounds (e.g. *soft silk, wind whistles*)

Short phrases for rhythm and interest

Freedom with language—words and grammar used in unusual ways

What did you read?

1. Circle the best answer. In the first poem what experience is being described?
   - a Mum tucking you into bed at night
   - b Mum making the bed while you lie on it
   - c Watching Mum make the bed

2. Write the same word in both spaces. In the second poem, the poet cleverly links the idea of ______________ off to sleep and a boat ______________ on the water.

3. In the second poem, why would piling on more blankets ***cook up*** dreams? ______________

   ____

4. Circle two correct answers. The third poem is about:
   - a riding fast
   - b riding slow
   - c riding to school
   - d riding after school

5. In the first poem, the poet repeats the ***s*** and ***sh*** sound (e.g. ***shut***, ***soft silk***, ***brushes***, ***sheet***, ***settles***) to suggest the softness of the sheet. (This is called **alliteration**.) In the third poem, she repeats the ***w*** sound in ***wind whistles***. What does the ***w*** sound suggest? ______________

6. Can you write one word to express how the child feels at the end of each poem?
   - a "I lie straight" ______________
   - b "Drifting off" ______________
   - c "My bike" ______________

How were they written?

1. The poet uses interesting verbs to describe action and movement.
   - a In the first poem, which verbs are used instead of these more common ones?
     touches ______________ falls ______________ covers ______________
   - b In the third poem, which *two* verbs are used to describe travelling fast?
     ______________ ______________

2. Poets often use similes—saying one thing is like another—to give us a clear image of what they mean. What does the poet say that these things are like?
   - a The feel of the sheet (poem 1): ______________
   - b The way she lies on winter nights (poem 2): ______________
   - c The way she goes off to sleep (poem 2): ______________

3. Poets often use a phrase or single word instead of a full sentence to express an idea. They might do this to help the rhythm or to 'sharpen' the image they want to convey.
   - a In the third poem, write the short phrase used instead of:
     - i It is dusk: ______________
     - ii The path is smooth: ______________
     - iii The tyres of my bike hum: ______________
     - iv I don't use my hands: ______________
     - v I've got a tailwind now: ______________
   - b Circle the best answer. These short phrases and single words create an image of:
     slowness bumpiness speed happiness

4. All the poems are about subjects that most children would be familiar with. Which one did you like most and why? ______________

   ____

Spelling and meaning

straight	breeze	whisper	search	curled
bruises	quiet	gently	caught	whistles
smooth	tyres	swooping	through	possums

Homophones are words that sound the same but are spelt differently. Some words in the word box have homophones. Look at these two phrases:

The quiet night (quiet = silent)

Feeling quite content (quite = completely)

Note: ***quite*** can also mean 'rather' or 'a little' (e.g. ***quite tall*** = tall, but not very tall).

1 Choose the correct homophone to put into these sentences. Use your dictionary if you need to.

a I swam strongly ________________ the waves. (through, threw)

b He ________________ the boomerang. (through, threw)

c I never ________________ of the sound of the surf. (tyre, tire)

d The bike ________________ goes bang. (tyre, tire)

e The ball goes ________________ through the hoop. (straight, strait)

f The islands are separated by a narrow ________________ (straight, strait)

g The netball ________________ is filled with cheers. (caught, court)

h I ________________ up with the runners just in time. (caught, court)

2 The vowel sounds in English words are often the hardest to get right, especially if two vowels are used together.

a Underline the vowels (or letters such as ***y*** that make a vowel sound) in the words in the word box.

b Learn them using the **look–say–cover–write–check** method.

c **Without looking back**, fill in the missing vowels from these tricky word box words.

BR ___ ___ Z ___	STR ___ ___ GHT	S ___ ___ RCH	P ___ SS ___ MS
THR ___ ___ GH	SW ___ ___ PING	T ___ R ___ S	BR ___ ___ S ___ S
Q ___ ___ ___ T	C ___ ___ GHT	C ___ RL ___ D	SM ___ ___ TH

3 Many ***wh-*** words describe sounds, for example ***whisper***, ***whistles***. This makes them very useful when writing poems.

Use your dictionary to look up these words. Then, next to each one, write something that would make that sound. (There are many possible answers.)

a whack ________________

b wham ________________

c wheeze ________________

d whimper ________________

e whine ________________

f whinge ________________

g whip ________________

h whirr ________________

i whiz ________________

j whoop ________________

Grammar—Similes and metaphors

Similes and metaphors are types of **figurative language**—language that is used in an unusual way to express the way something looks, sounds, feels, smells, tastes, moves or behaves.
Similes and metaphors help you to create a picture or **image** for your reader or listener. In a **simile**, one thing is compared to another using ***like*** or ***as … as***.

Examples I drift like a boat …
… curled up like a fox.
The sky is as soft as a blanket …

In a **metaphor**, one thing is said to actually **be** the other thing.

Examples I am a boat …
I am a fox …
The sky is a soft blanket …

1 Look at these students' similes. Can you make up a different simile to suggest the same image?

a As rich as a Lotto winner: ______

b As boring as my brother's friends: ______

c As unimportant as a speck of pepper: ______

d As green as broccoli: ______

e As strong as my father's coffee: ______

f As cool as a fresh sheet: ______

g As warm as a pair of mittens: ______

h As loud as an alarm clock: ______

i As hot as lava: ______

2 Below are the beginnings and endings of some students' metaphors. Can you work out which go with which? You might have different ideas from the students who wrote these, but that is OK—as long as the metaphors you make mean something to you.

a The wind is	torture.
b Sleep is	freedom.
c Dancing is	a soft cocoon.
d Chocolate cake is	a whip.
e Exams are	heaven.

Punctuation—Punctuating poems

In poetry we have more **freedom with punctuation** than in other writing. Sometimes we use it the usual way to break up ideas and make our meaning clear. However, we can also use punctuation to actually suggest the ideas, images or feelings we are writing about.

1 Go back to "I lie straight" and look at the punctuation. Then read the poem out loud.

a How did the lack of punctuation make you read the poem? In a smooth, flowing way? A snappy, stop-start way? ______

b What connection can you see between the punctuation and the subject of the poem?

______

c Why do you think the poet has not put a full stop at the end? ______

______

2 Now go back to "My bike" and look at the punctuation. Then read the poem out loud.

a How did the lack of punctuation make you read the poem? Quickly? Slowly?

____

b What connection can you see between the punctuation and the subject of the poem?

____

c The poet uses one punctuation mark at the end of the poem. What is the effect of this single exclamation mark? ______________________________

3 Can you help this student punctuate her poem so that it helps to suggest the experience described? (There is no right answer—there are many possibilities.) Before you add punctuation, read the poem out loud a few times.

Summer at the pool
splash
down down
straighten out now
what a dive
sweet sweet coolness
up now up
floating like driftwood
thick silent peace
mmmm
splash
peace over
time for fun

Can you help?

In the poems on page 18 you saw examples of alliteration—the repetition of similar consonant sounds to suggest an idea or image (e.g. ***soft silk***, ***brushes***, ***sheet***, ***settles***, ***wind whistles***).

In the following lines the students had some fun with alliteration after reading *Animalia* by Graeme Base. (If you don't know this fantastic book, have a look for it in your school or local library!)

Seven sly snails slithered slowly to Sydney.
Twenty tigers tip-toed through thousands of taipans typing true tales.
Five fan-tailed fish fight fiercely for food.
Two turtles talk to ten tarantulas.
Leaping leopards laugh at loping lions.
Lazy leopards lie luxuriously in the lolly shaped sun.
Six silly seals sing swinging sixties songs.
Black bats bash brick buildings.
Pink pigs play poker.
Ten termites tasted ten tinted timber tables.

Can you make up your own lines about different kinds of animals? If you can, use letters that suggest something about the animal (e.g. their speed, their sounds). Write your lines in the space below and add illustrations if you wish.

Puzzle time

Can you match these characters from well-known poems to their actions?

Belinda	Matilda	the Owl and the Pussycat	my mother	an old woman
Jack	Isabel	Wynken, Blinken and Nod	the Jumblies	the Pobble

Which one:

- **a** swallowed a fly? ______
- **b** built a house? ______
- **c** met an enormous bear, but didn't care? ______
- **d** said you should never play with the gypsies in the wood? ______
- **e** went to sea in a beautiful pea-green boat? ______
- **f** sailed off in a wooden shoe one night? ______
- **g** went to sea in a sieve? ______
- **h** has no toes, but once had as many as we? ______
- **i** told such dreadful lies, it made one gasp and stretch one's eyes? ______
- **j** lived in a little white house with a little black kitten and a little grey mouse, and a little yellow dog and a little red wagon and a realio, trulio, little pet dragon? ______

DID YOU KNOW?

A poet called Ogden Nash is famous for his short, witty poems. One is called "The Fly":

The Lord in his wisdom made the fly,
And then forgot to tell us why.

Your turn to write

Tips for particularly powerful poets

- Read lots of poetry! There are many terrific poets who write especially for children—for example, Elizabeth Honey, Bill Condon, Steven Herrick, Max Fatchen, Robin Klein, Doug McLeod, Michael Dugan and Michael Rosen. Check out these poets in your school or local library and ask for help to find others.
- Read your own poems out loud as you are writing them to see how they sound. You'll find out which words work and which words don't. And remember, poems don't have to rhyme. Rhyming can help to give a poem rhythm and beat but it can also make you write thoughts and ideas that just don't make sense.

1 The poems on page 18 are about ordinary, everyday experiences, but the poet wrote about these experiences in a way that made us appreciate how enjoyable they are. (I especially liked "I lie straight" because it reminded me of something I loved doing when I was a child.)

Try writing a poem about an everyday experience you know well. Follow these steps.

a Choose your topic. Here are some suggestions, but you might want to write about another experience. Be sure it is something you especially like, or especially don't like.

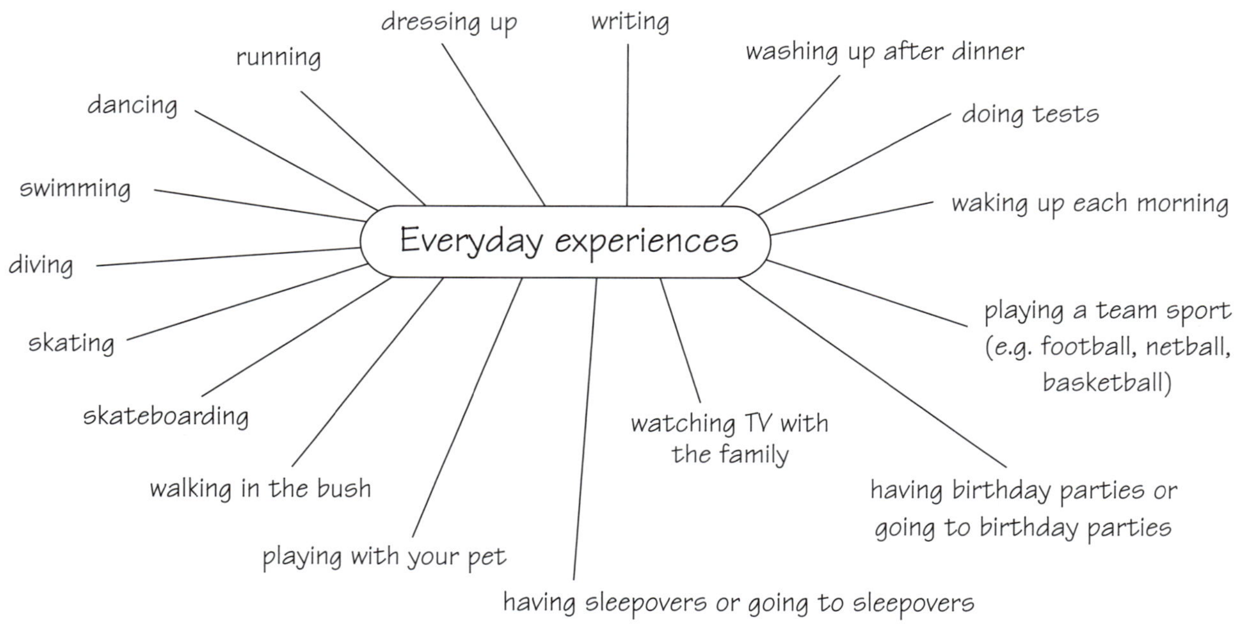

b Now think long and hard about your topic. Close your eyes and imagine you are doing it (e.g. dancing, running, swimming) right now. Use the following questions to jot down some ideas.

What is the experience?

When does it take place? Where?

What do you see?

What do you hear?

What do you smell or taste?

What do you touch?

How do you move?

Are there other people involved? Who?

What is good or bad about the experience?

What is funny or interesting about it?

How does the experience make you feel?

Why do you love or hate the experience?

c Draft your poem in the space below.

- Use words and images to help your reader understand your ideas.
- Use phrases instead of full sentences to help the rhythm and sharpen images.
- Use rhyme *only* if it helps to express an idea.
- Use punctuation to suggest or emphasise ideas.
- Read your poem out loud a few times as you write and see how it sounds.
- Revise it if needed till you are happy with it, and check your spelling.
- Write it out neatly and draw a good picture to go with it. Put it up where people will see it.

2 Are you ready for one more poem? Choose one of the other everyday experiences listed in activity 1 or think of one of your own. Follow the same three steps. This time, write your poem on your own paper or in your Writer's Notebook.

Answers on pages 92–93

Chapter 4 Writing a procedural recount

The aim of a procedural recount is to record the steps taken to achieve a goal or do a task. A procedural recount is like a procedure because it tells how to do something, but it is also like a factual recount, because it tells what you did *after* you did it.

STRUCTURE

LANGUAGE

These students had to construct a model of a city of the future using recycled garbage and then write a recount of how they made it.

Sea-city

Statement about the goal or task

1. Our group decided that our city of the future would be a city in the sea, because we already have the materials and technology for this kind of city. Oil rigs, for example, are basically mini-cities in the sea.

Comments on what worked well and what did not work well

2. Our design had three levels (see sketch below). We used the sides of an enormous cardboard box measuring approximately 90 cm by 60 cm to make the floors of each level. We tried using cardboard cylinders as support pillars between the floors, but they would not stick properly. Then we found lots of pieces of polystyrene, which were all the same height, so we used them instead.

Steps taken in the order they occurred

3. We started by using strong glue to stick six pieces of the polysterene onto one piece of cardboard. We then turned the whole thing upside down and stood it in the ocean made from dark blue tissue paper. In the actual city, the pillars would go right down to the seabed.

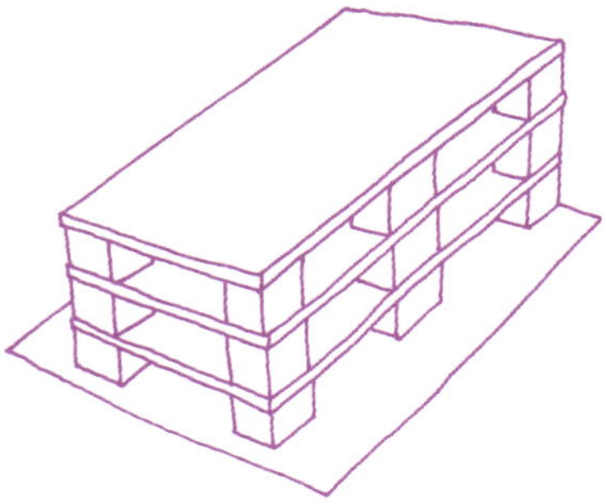

4. The first level of our city was for services like sewerage, water, electricity, air conditioning and gas. So we filled up the space with thin rubber tubing as pipes and bubble wrap as insulation. These materials looked very realistic. We stuck on six more polystyrene blocks to support the next level of flooring, and then fixed another piece of cardboard on top.

5. Then we worked on the second level, which was for factories and storage. We made the factories out of boxes and used some tin cans as storage silos and tanks. We put people made out of pipe cleaners and some matchbox transport vehicles all around to show how people would work in these areas. We added more pillars.

6. Next, we made the third level—the living area. We used plastic packaging from Easter eggs to make dome-shaped shops, service centres and sports centres. We made the housing out of boxes. We kept the housing areas low because we didn't think tall skyscrapers would be suitable out at sea. We built a monorail with wire, foil and hooks. We didn't think people would use cars in a sea-city.

7. Finally, we used some clear plastic biscuit packaging to make lifts and moving walkways along each side of the city. We also taped some plastic sheeting along one side to represent one wall, but in the real city there would be four thick glass walls.

Evaluation or interpretation of results

8. We decided it would have been better if we had made a few cities all connected across the water by a system of covered tunnels. Otherwise we were happy with the way our city turned out. We were worried that it would collapse but it didn't, because we only used lightweight objects on top of the cardboard floors.

Action verbs

Precise language to show exactly what was done (e.g. measurements, materials)

Past tense

Time words and expressions

Adjectives to describe things

Common nouns and pronouns to describe materials and processes

What did you read?

1. Circle the best answer. Why did the students decide to build a sea-city?
   - a Because they like oil rigs
   - b Because it would be possible for humans to build sea-cities
   - c Because they thought a sea-city would be easy
2. What were the three levels of the city for?

   Level 1: ______________________________

   Level 2: ______________________________

   Level 3: ______________________________
3. What materials did the students use for these parts of the city?
   - a floors: ______________
   - b support pillars: ______________
   - c ocean: ______________
   - d electricity and gas pipes: ______________
   - e insulation: ______________
   - f sports centres: ______________
   - g city walls: ______________
   - h lifts and walkways: ______________
4. True or false?
   - a The students were totally happy with their city. ________
   - b The students were worried the city might collapse. ________
   - c The city did collapse. ________
5. Draw a quick picture of the students' idea for an improvement to their city. Use your own paper or your Writer's Notebook.

How was it written?

1. In which paragraph do the students tell us:
   - a their goal? __________
   - b the overall structure of their city? __________
2. The students tell us what they did in the O ___ ___ ___ ___ they did it. Underline the words at the beginning of the paragraphs that give us information about this.
3. Procedural recounts often say why certain steps were taken. What reasons did the students give in paragraph 6 for:
   - a making the housing low? ______________________________
   - b building a monorail? ______________________________
4. A procedural recount usually ends with an evaluation of the procedure—what was good or bad about it. Was the students' evaluation overall positive or negative? ______________
5. If you were going to build a sea-city model just like this one, would this procedural recount be (tick one):

   very useful ____ quite useful ____ useless ____

   Give your reasons. ______________________________

   ____

Spelling and meaning

decided	materials	basically	design	measuring
approximately	cylinders	pieces	height	electricity
realistic	silos	vehicles	skyscrapers	lightweight

Tip for simply superb spellers
Think about the meaning of a word before you spell it to avoid mistakes. For example, if you think of ***electriC*** you will remember the soft ***c*** in ***electriCity***.

1 Can you complete these word families based on words in the word box?

a BAS ___ C (adjective) B ___ S ___ S (noun) BAS ___ M ___ ___ T (noun)
b E ___ ___ ___T ___ ___ C (adjective) E ___ ___ ___ ___ R ___ C ___ L (adjective)
EL ___ ___ TR ___ FY (verb)
c UNR ___ ___ ___ (adjective) UN ___ ___ ___ ___ IST ___ ___ (adjective)
RE ___ L ___ T ___ (noun)

2 Fill in the blanks with words from the word box.

a opposite of heavy: ________________
b opposite of exactly: ________________
c cylindrical tanks: ________________
d very tall buildings: ________________
e really: ________________
f a measurement: ________________
g plan for building: ________________
h things, stuff, objects: ________________
i a kind of power: ________________
j seeming real: ________________
k transporters: ________________
l made a decision: ________________
m working out size: ________________
n round tube-shaped objects: ________________

Learn any words you had trouble with using the **look–say–cover–write–check** method.

Weight and ***wait*** are **homophones**—words that sound the same but are spelt differently.
Example We wanted to wait till we were sure it would work.
The weight of the wood kept the support pillars steady.

3 Choose the correct homophones to use in these sentences. Use your dictionary if you need to.

a We were not sure ________________ (whether/weather) to use plastic or paper.
b The ________________ (whether/weather) would affect life in a sea-city.
c We were only ________________ (aloud/allowed) to use recycled materials.
d We read our recounts ________________ (aloud/allowed) to the class.
e We knew ________________ (witch/which) material would be strongest.
f They made a ________________ (witch/which) in their craft lesson.
g Sound insulation would be needed to keep the area ________________ (quiet/quite).
h We only needed one ________________ (piece/peace) of cardboard.
i Finally there was ________________ (piece/peace) in the classroom.
j The ________________ (bored/board) was too heavy to use.
k We got ________________ (bored/board) waiting for everyone to finish.

Grammar—Verbs and verb groups

The **verb** is the core of the clause or sentence. It tells us what is happening.
You probably know that a verb is a **doing word**—a word that tells us what someone or something is doing (e.g. ***build***, ***cut***, ***use***, ***work***, ***make***).
However, not all verbs are about *doing* something. Verbs can also be about:
saying (e.g. ***ask***, ***comment***, ***declare***, ***shout***)
thinking and feeling (e.g. ***decide***, ***imagine***, ***believe***, ***hurt***, ***surprise***)
relating (e.g. ***be***, ***have***, ***involve***, ***belong***).

A verb can be one word (e.g. ***build***), but sometimes we need other words (**auxiliary** or helper verbs) (e.g. ***is building***, ***has been building***, ***was built***, ***could build***). We call the whole group of words the **verb group**.
Sometimes we need a few words to express the verb idea. Look at these verb groups from the text:

We **tried using** cardboard cylinders.
We **started by using** strong glue.
We **filled up** the space with thin rubber tubing.

1 Can you put these verb groups into the procedural recount below?

managed to hold up	could hold up	tried to hold up	was
had to span	were asked to construct	held up	made

Bridge Building
By Chris Davies and Stephen Pitt

In Term 2 Class 6M ______________________ a bridge out of paper that ______________ as much weight as possible. The bridge ______________ ______________ a distance of 10 centimetres. Chris Learned's was the best. Chris ______________ 1 kilogram without his paper collapsing. Other students who ______________ 1 kilogram failed because of their design. Chris ______________ his bridge with a section shaped like an unused staple. Our bridge ______________ 375 grams which ______________ the second largest mass.

2 Try to avoid using the same verbs all the time. Some common verbs you might use in a procedural recount are on the left. Fill in the missing letters for their synonyms on the right.

a	stick	=	G ___ ___ ___	T ___ ___ ___	F ___ ___
b	make	=	B ___ ___ ___ D	C ___ NS ___ ___ ___ T	
c	start	=	B ___ ___ ___ N	C ___ M ___ ___ ___ ___ E	
d	turn	=	R ___ T ___ ___ E	T ___ ___ ___ T	INV ___ ___ T
e	put	=	P ___ ___ ___ E	S ___ ___ ND	
f	watch	=	V ___ ___ W	O ___ SER ___ ___	

Punctuation—Hyphens

We can use **hyphens** (-) to **join two or more words** to make a new word or expression (e.g. ***sea-city***, ***dome-shaped***, ***mini-cities***).
We sometimes use hyphens in compound words (e.g. ***make-up***, ***well-known***, ***hold-up***), but if the word has been used for a long time, we leave out the hyphen (e.g. ***skyscraper***, ***cardboard***).

It can be difficult to know when to use a hyphen, so it is usually best to look up a word in the dictionary if you are not sure.
Note: We also use hyphens to break a long word at the end of a line. Try to avoid this, but if you need to, always break the word after a syllable.

Where would you add hyphens in these sentences?

a Another group used odd shaped pieces of polystyrene as city sculptures.
b We wanted to make a city that would be useful in both ice cold and red hot weather conditions.
c Jake's group built a multi storey city like ours but it was underground.
d We had to re use things we had at home.
e Zaara's group constructed an eight sided city.
f The best model had six multi purpose levels.

NUMBERS

Follow these rules when writing numbers:

- Write the word if the number is ten or less (e.g. *three* cylinders).
- Use figures where the number is a measurement (e.g. *90* cm).
- Write words instead of numbers at the start of sentences (e.g. *Nineteen* models were displayed).

Can you help?

Can you help put these students' procedural recount back in the right order?

Building Towers
By Mercia Hamilton and Erin Wilson Leary

a ______ The tower had to be rigid and stand up by itself.
b ______ We did this process four times and then decided to strengthen the tower by doubling the newspaper.
c ______ Our task was to build a tower using only ten sheets of newspaper and sticky tape.
d ______ We also used tape to stick the tower to the table.
e ______ The tallest free standing tower would be the winner.
f ______ When Mr Guilfoyle measured the towers, ours was three metres high and was the winning tower.
g ______ It was very thin but very rigid.
h ______ Our idea was to tightly roll the paper into tubes.

Puzzle time

1 Can you unscramble these **shape** adjectives? Remember that you are looking for an adjective, not a noun, so in the first example the answer is ***cylindrical*** not ***cylinder***.

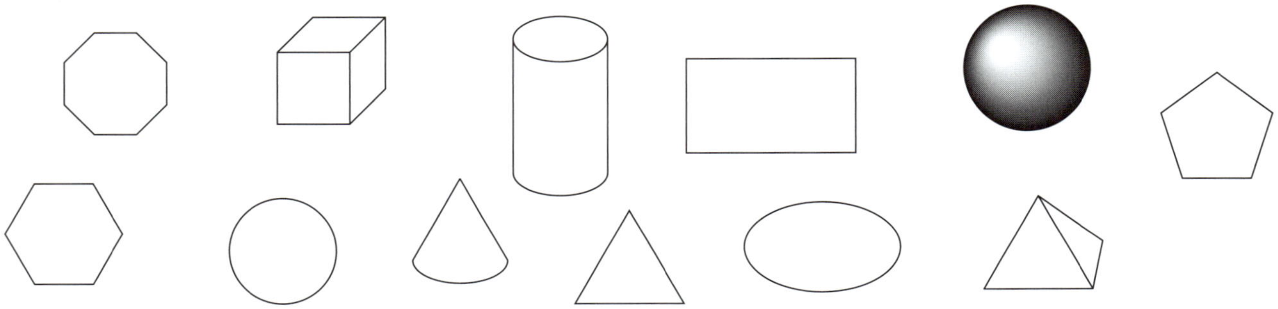

a YLCCINDRILA ____________________

b LARREANGUCT ____________________

c HECALSPRI ____________________

d AOVL ____________________

e NILCOCA ____________________

f MRAIDPY-SHAPED ____________________

g BCUCI ____________________

h IRCCARUL ____________________

i NLIAARTRGU ____________________

j OAGALCTON ____________________

k EXHANALGO ____________________

l PTANONALGE ____________________

2 Speaking of the sea and sea-cities, do you know:

a the name of the mythical city that is thought to have sunk into the sea in ancient times? (*Hint:* It starts with A.) ___ ___ ___ ___ ___ ___ ___ ___

b the name of the Roman god of the sea, starting with N (also a planet)? ___ ___ ___ ___ ___ ___ ___

c the name of the Greek god of the sea, starting with P and ending with N?

___ ___ ___ ___ ___ ___ ___ ___

Your turn to write

Tips for completely crafty writers

- Before you start a procedural recount, make notes of the steps you took *in the order* you took them. Then write your recount in this order.
- Try to be as precise as you can so that your readers will know exactly what you did.

1 A procedural recount is like a procedure. However:

- you write what *you* did, NOT what *someone else should* do;
- at the end you write a comment which evaluates or interprets your experience.

Read this procedure about a simple scientific experiment.

If you can, do the experiment and then write a procedural recount about it on page 32.

If you can't do the experiment, just use the information in the procedure to make up your recount.

- Don't list the equipment at the start. Just include the equipment in the steps you took.
- Use numbers for the steps if you think this will make it clearer.

Why do some things float and some sink?

You will need

a large clear-plastic container, a jug, a large spoon, honey, oil and things to float (e.g. whole nuts, dried pasta, grapes, small metal objects, Lego bricks)

Instructions

1. Pour the honey over the back of the spoon into the container, until it is a quarter full (about 4 or 5 cm).
2. Slowly pour the same amount of vegetable oil into the container. Then add the same amount of water.
3. Wait until the liquids settle into layers. Then drop the objects in and see what happens.

So what happened?

Did the liquids separate into three layers—honey on the bottom, then water and then oil? This happens because some liquids are lighter or denser than others.

What happened to your objects? Did some sink? Did some float?

And where did they float? On the honey? On the water? On the oil? The objects will float if they are lighter than the liquid.

Statement of the task or goal of the procedure

Steps you took to do the task or achieve the goal

Evaluation

2 Think of something you have built or made—by yourself or with others. Here are some suggestions:

- a billy cart
- a cubby house
- a tower or bridge or other structure
- a garden
- a campfire
- an ant farm
- an insect trap
- a kite
- a meal for your family
- a cake.

Make notes under the headings below and then write your procedural recount in your Writer's Notebook. Remember: we want to know what you did, and what worked and didn't work.

Goal or task (What were you trying to do? Who was involved? What was the overall plan or idea?)

Steps taken (What did you do? In what order? Remember to number the steps.)

Evaluation (What did you learn? What did the procedure prove? How did you enjoy the experience?)

Answers on page 93

Chapter 5 Writing a letter of opinion (exposition)

In a letter of opinion, your aim is to convince the reader of your point of view using facts and logical arguments. A letter of opinion is a kind of exposition.

STRUCTURE

- ***Your address* and date***
- ***Name, title and address of person you are writing to***
- ***Greeting***
- ***Introduction*** to topic of letter, reason for writing and point of view
- ***Logical arguments*** to support opinion
- ***Personal experiences*** to support opinion
- ***Ending***—repeating purpose of letter
- ***Sign off*** showing respect
- ***Name and signature***

35 WXXXXXX Rd
Balmain, 2035
23rd March, 2004

Ms Sandra Nori
NSW Member for Port Jackson
22 NXXXXXXX St
LXXXXXXX, 2035

Dear Ms Nori,

My name is Joe Brown. I am 11 years old and I live in Balmain. I am writing to you because I love skateboarding just like all **my friends** in the area you're in charge of. We need your help because a lot of adults in this area have tried to stop a skateboarding ramp being built in the Mort Bay Redevelopment. They think young people will just gather there and make a mess. **I think** they're being **mean** and **selfish**.

There are many good reasons for a skateboarding ramp. Firstly, skateboarding is a lot of fun for kids. **Also** it will improve their skill and fitness, and keep them off the narrow and dangerous roads of Balmain. **Besides**, a skateboarding ramp would be a great place to make new friends. THIS WOULD BE GREAT FOR THE COMMUNITY!

I have skated at Avalon skateboarding ramp with some good mates. It's a great ramp designed by the local skateboarders, where big kids help little kids to skateboard, and where parents are happy to take their kids because it's a safe place.

If you can help put this skateboard ramp in, **us kids** will be very grateful.

With best wishes and lots of hope,

Joe Brown

Joe Brown

* We have blocked out the actual addresses for privacy reasons.

LANGUAGE

- ***Polite, respectful language***
- ***Personal language***
- ***Opinion adjectives***
- ***Connectives*** to link ideas
- ***Mostly formal language*** but some ***informal language*** is also acceptable
- Mostly ***present tense***

What did you read?

1. What does Joe want Ms Nori to do? ____________________

____

2. Circle the best answer. How does Ms Nori have the power to help?
   - **a** She is an adult.
   - **b** She is a famous skateboarder.
   - **c** She is a politician.
3. Circle the best answer. Who has stopped the skateboard ramp being built, according to Joe?
   - **a** The people at the Mort Bay Redevelopment
   - **b** Adults who live in the area
   - **c** Young people who make a mess
4. How many arguments does Joe put forward to support his opinion?

____

5. Which argument do you think is Joe's strongest, and why? ____________________

____

6. Name one good point about Avalon skateboard ramp. ____________________

____

How was it written?

1. Joe writes "I love skateboarding <u>just like all my friends</u>", "<u>we</u> need your help" and "<u>us kids</u> will be very grateful". Why do you think he does this? Circle the best answer.
   - **a** Because his friends won't write letters
   - **b** Because there are many children in the area
   - **c** Because he wants to show he is not the only one who wants a ramp
2. Joe lists many good reasons for building a skateboard ramp. Why do you think he has put his last reason in capital letters? ____________________

____

3. Personal experiences can be helpful in letters of opinion. Why do you think Joe thought it would help to mention his experience of the Avalon skateboarding ramp? Circle the best answer.
   - **a** Because it is his favourite place to skate and his parents like it too
   - **b** Because it is an example of a skateboard ramp that has been good for the community
   - **c** Because it has been designed by local skateboarders
4. Circle the best answer. Why do you think it is a good idea to repeat the purpose of the letter at the end?
   - **a** To remind Ms Nori in case she has forgotten
   - **b** To be polite
   - **c** To make his letter more persuasive
5. Do you think that Ms Nori would be influenced by Joe's letter? Why or why not? ____________________

____

Spelling and meaning

because	skateboarding	friends	area	built
there	reasons	improve	their	narrow
they're	dangerous	community	designed	grateful

The word box contains three words often confused: ***there***, ***their***, ***they're***.

- ***There*** means a place (e.g. over there). It is also for expressions like ***there is***.
  Example There are many good reasons for a skateboarding ramp.
  You can USUALLY replace ***there*** with ***here*** and the sentence still makes sense.
- ***Their*** means "of them".
  Example Also it will improve their skill and fitness (the skill and fitness of them).
  You can USUALLY replace ***their*** with "of them".
- ***They're*** means "they are".
  Example They're being mean and selfish.
  You can ALWAYS replace ***they're*** with "they are".

1 Choose ***there***, ***their*** or ***they're*** to use in these sentences.

a The girls would like ________________ soccer team to win the competition.

b ________________ playing at the local sports centre.

c ________________ are three good arguments for building an outdoor pool.

d I think ________________ would be many people with the same opinion.

e ________________ playing all ________________ games over ________________.

2 **Antonyms** are words that have opposite meanings (e.g. ***dangerous*** and ***safe***). Many antonyms are made by adding a prefix (e.g. ***un***, ***in***, ***im***). Can you make the antonyms of these words by adding one of these prefixes?

a grateful ________________

b significant ________________

c selfish ________________

d mobile ________________

e perfect ________________

f personal ________________

g polite ________________

h impressive ________________

i active ________________

j adequate ________________

k direct ________________

l effective ________________

3 Many words are made by combining two words. The new word is a **compound word**. What compound words can you make by adding a word *before* or *after* the following words?

a board: ________________________________

b snow: ________________________________

c surf: ________________________________

d wind: ________________________________

Grammar—Opinion adjectives

In letters of opinion, we often use adjectives that clearly show what that opinion is. For example, we might say that a local council decision is ***great***, ***terrific*** or ***beneficial***. Of course other people might call the same decision ***ridiculous***, ***useless*** or ***harmful***.
These kinds of adjectives are called **opinion adjectives**. They are useful because they can influence the reader to agree with our point of view.
However, we need to use them with care—especially negative ones. They can give the impression that we are very emotional about the issue and so not thinking clearly. They can also be insulting, for example, if you say someone's idea is ***stupid*** or ***idiotic***.

1 Underline the adjective that tells the writer's opinion in each sentence below.

a The ramp would be a sensible way to use the money saved when the pool closed.
b The beautiful bushland behind my house is home to many kinds of wildlife.
c A new school library would be a brilliant way to get more kids to read.
d All the children would be very sad if you closed the after school care centre.
e The parade is the most entertaining part of the Gala Day.
f Making the old tennis courts into a car park is a very boring idea.

2 It is a good idea to vary the opinion adjectives you use. Below are some words you could use instead of the opinion adjectives at the top of the column. Can you unscramble them? (The first letter is in bold.)

GOOD (e.g. plan, action, idea)	BAD (e.g. plan, action, idea)	BEAUTIFUL (e.g. building, landscape)	UGLY (e.g. building, landscape)
PSOTIEVI	S**U**ESSEL	LOR**G**OUSI	N**U**ATTRCATVIE
BRLLNTIAI	**U**NELPHFUL	**G**GROSEOU	**R**ETOLVGNI
SE**U**LUF	**S**HKCONGI	TTA**A**RCTEIV	**U**NEAPSLANT
X**E**CLLENTE	GE**N**ATVIE	DID**S**LPEN	E**T**RRBLIE
L**C**VERE	FLU**H**ARM	GA**M**NIFITENC	SI**D**GSTUING

Punctuation—Dates and it's/its

It is important to **write the date** correctly in letters. Joe writes:
23rd March, 2004
He could have written:
March 23rd, 2004 or *23 March, 2004*
March 23, 2004 or *23/3/04 (or 23-3-04)*
Even though we **say** "the 23rd of March", we don't **write** it this way.

1 Write down these dates in one of the ways above. Use a different way for each date.

Your birthdate: ______________________

The birthdate of a family member: ______________________

Your best friend's birthdate: ____________________

Christmas Day next year: ____________________

New Year's Day last year: ____________________

It's and ***its*** are easy to confuse but just remember these two things:

- ***It's*** ALWAYS ALWAYS ALWAYS means "it is" or "it has". ("It has" is less common.)
- ***Its*** is a word meaning "belonging to it" (just like ***hers*** means "belonging to her").

Examples It's a great ramp. (= It is a great ramp.)
It's been there for two years. (= It has been there for two years.)
I have an idea for its location. (= I have an idea for the location of it.)

So, only use ***it's*** if you can replace it with "it is" or "it has" and the sentence still makes sense.

2 Fill in the blanks with ***it's*** or ***its***. Remember: only use ***it's*** if you can replace it with "it is" or "it has".

a I believe ______________ a really terrible plan.

b The group wants you to know ______________ honest opinion.

c Most people who object to ______________ construction don't know the facts.

d One thousand people say ______________ an excellent place for a skatepark.

e Its success will depend on ______________ size, ______________ design and ______________ location.

f ______________ been talked about for long enough. ______________ time for action.

Can you help?

Joy wrote this letter to the editor of her local newspaper, but I've muddled up the order of her sentences. Can you put them back the right way? Number them from 1 to 5.

Dear Editor,

__ Nearly every netball game, someone slips over. There have been some serious injuries because people have slipped over.

__ Many people have complained about this before and I think it's time someone did something about it.

__ This should not keep happening. Someone should do something about it. They should rip up the old grass and lay down new grass. They could put a cover or something over the courts because the main reason there is no grass is because the rain washes it away.

__ In fact, you could even ask one of my friends who tripped over in a game and twisted her knee. She had to have an operation to put it back in place. She couldn't play for the rest of the season. It is very painful and she has to use crutches.

__ I am writing to complain that the Lapstone grass netball courts are in a terrible condition. There is sand and dirt everywhere.

Joy Tarasenko, Glenbrook

With permission, Joy Tarasenko and *Blue Mountains Gazette*

Puzzle time

How much do you know about where sports are played? You'll find a few places in this crossword.

Across:

3. Joe wants one of these, but they are used in other sports too.
6. You might even have one of these in your backyard.
7. Lots of 6 across together make an ______________ centre.
8. Might be made of grass or clay or a synthetic surface.
9. You need two wheels for this speedy place beginning with V.
13. Another speedy place but this time you will be on your feet—unless you fall over!
14. Ten pins are used in the sport played in this place.
16. Row, row, row your boat … at the ______________ centre.
17. This word is used in many sports. You might be familiar with one with obstacles?

Down:

1. Horses run around this but humans do too in other sports.
2. A big place used for athletics and other major events
4. Important in cricket—very hard!
6. Take a big jump into this and sand will fly.
10. Another word for a golf course
11. An egg-shaped place for sport or just running around
12. You will find parallel bars, rings and trampolines here.
13. Bullets fly at the shooting __________.
15. Many indoor games are played on this.

Your turn to write

Tip for electrically effective letter writers

When writing a letter to persuade someone to do something, remember to be polite as well as clear. You do not want the person to be insulted by the words you use. If they are, they are unlikely to agree with you or do what you want.

1. Writing opinion letters is one way that ordinary people can influence what happens in their neighbourhood, community, state or country. Imagine you wanted to write about the issues below. Who would you write to? Draw lines from the issue to the person or organisation—possibly more than one.

a A plan to close the local swimming pool	Local newspaper
b People dumping rubbish into a local river	Major newspaper
c People throwing cigarette butts on the street	Local Council member or mayor
d A plan to build houses on bushland near your house	Local member of state/territory Parliament
e Whether or not we should be a republic	State premier or territory chief minister
f Extending the summer school holidays	Local member of federal Parliament
g The need for new facilities (e.g. library, buildings, sports areas) at your school	Member of Parliament in charge of an area (e.g. education, environment)
	Prime minister

2. Imagine you want now to write about one of the above topics. Use your own ideas and imagination to complete the skeleton letter below. (Just make up a name for the person you are writing to, if you do not know it.)

____________________ (Your address and the date)

____

____

____

____________________ (Title/address of person you are writing to)

____

____

Dear ____________________,

I am writing about ____________________

____

____

____

____

I think/I don't think ____________________

____

____

____

____

____

Here are ____________ very good reasons. ______________________________

____

____

____

____

____

____

____

____

____

____

____

____

This issue is really important to me and ______________________________

so I hope ____

____

____

____

____

Thank you

Yours sincerely

____

3 I am sure there is an issue in your local area that affects you (e.g. sports or other facilities for young people). Write a letter to the local newspaper or to your local Council member giving your opinion. Use your own paper.

Remember:

- Write your address, the date and the title and address of the person you are writing to.
- Say why you are writing.
- State your opinion clearly.
- Give some reasons to support your opinion.
- Add any personal experiences that support your opinion.
- Conclude by repeating why you are writing.
- Sign off with words that show your thanks and respect.

You will need to write your letter out again very neatly, and make sure the spelling, punctuation and grammar are correct, before you send it.

Answers on pages 93–95

Chapter 6 Writing an information report

In an information report, your aim is to give your audience factual information on a topic. Many reports are about groups of things (e.g. stars), but some are about one particular thing (e.g. the Moon).

STRUCTURE

LANGUAGE

Stars

What are stars?

Stars are huge spheres of flaming gas. They are like huge nuclear furnaces. They throw out enormous quantities of light, heat and other forms of energy. The heat is unimaginable to us—around 15 million degrees Celsius. However, not all stars have the same amount of heat, and the difference can be seen by their colour. The hottest stars shine blue and after that, in order of heat, they shine white, yellow, orange and then red.

Our Sun

Our Sun is a star. It looks bigger to us than all the other stars in the sky, but this is only because it is the closest (about 150 million kilometres away) and the other stars are much further away. The next nearest, Alpha Centauri, is 4.3 light years away. (One light year is the distance that light travels in one year.) That means it is more than 40 million million kilometres away.

How stars are born

A star starts out as a cloud of hydrogen gas and dust. It begins to form when something makes it collapse in on itself with the force of gravity. As it collapses it begins to rotate and heat up. When the temperature gets high enough in the core (many millions of degrees) to set off nuclear reactions, it produces an enormous amount of energy and the star begins to shine. These reactions are the same as in hydrogen bombs only billions of times more powerful.

How long stars live

Astronomers have observed many stars at different stages and pieced information together to get a typical star's life span. However, not all stars live for the same length of time. That depends on their size. The biggest stars have short but spectacular lives. Middle-sized stars, like our own Sun, shine less brightly and die quietly, but they live longer—more than 5 billion years. The lightweight stars glow weakly but have a life measured in hundreds of billions of years.

How they die

A star begins to die when it runs out of hydrogen (its fuel). The helium core shrinks while its outer layers expand. Dying stars can sometimes produce strange phenomena such as supernovae (the result of massive stars exploding violently and brilliantly in the sky) and black holes (the result of massive stars collapsing and creating a solid area from which no light can escape).

Astronomers are constantly learning more about stars thanks to powerful telescopes, such as the Hubble Space Telescope, and space satellites that are able to travel further and further into our vast universe.

Structure notes:

Introduction to topic—often a definition, or the way the topic is classified

Information organised by sub-topics, in paragraphs and under headings

Topic sentences to help us understand main ideas

Sometimes ***explanations*** of how or why things happen

Factual information—not your opinions or personal experiences

Conclusion (not always needed)

Language notes:

Special, 'technical' words to talk about the topic

Often ***passive forms of verb*** to talk about processes

Definitions or explanations of terms readers might not understand

Usually ***present tense of verbs*** ('timeless present')

Mainly ***factual adjectives***

Topic word (*stars, a star*) repeated to link ideas

What did you read?

1. True or false?

   a All stars give out the same amount of heat. ________________

   b The Sun is the biggest star in our galaxy. ________________

   c The gas that fuels stars is hydrogen. ________________

   d Big stars live the longest. ________________

   e We are still learning more about stars. ________________

2. The nuclear reaction that produces stars is compared to ________________.

3. What does the colour of stars tell us? ________________

4. What unit of measurement is used to talk about huge distances? ________________

5. Circle the best answer. Stars are born:
   a when they run out of hydrogen and collapse.
   b when hydrogen and gas heats up and sets off a nuclear reaction.
   c when they get to a temperature of 15 million degrees.

How was it written?

1. Why do you think the writer defined 'stars'?
   a Because the reader might not have seen any stars
   b Because stars are very important objects in our universe
   c Because the reader might not know exactly what stars are

2. The writer repeats the word ***star*** or ***stars*** throughout the report in order to connect all the different facts. Underline each ***star*** or ***stars*** in the text and the headings. How many did you find altogether?

   ____

3. The information in "Stars" is clearly organised under headings. Under which headings would you add the three facts below?

   a Letters are used to classify stars. W is for the hottest blue star class. ________________

   b Light takes eight minutes to reach us from the Sun. __________________________

   c Some stars become what are known as 'red giants' as they die. __________________

4. The writer uses H ___ ___ ___ ___ ___ ___ S, P ___ ___ ___ ___ ___ ___ ___ ___ S and T ___ ___ ___ ___ S ___ ___ ___ ___ ___ ___ ___ ___ to help follow the main ideas.

5. These sentences were in the first report draft. Why do you think the writer took them out?
   I love to look up at the stars at night.
   Stars are more interesting than planets in my opinion.

   ____

6. These special scientific words are in the report. Tick those that are defined. Circle those that you would have liked definitions for.

   nuclear _______ Celsius _______ gravity _______

   light years _______ supernovae _______ black holes _______

Spelling and meaning

sphere	enormous	unimaginable	million	difference
collapse	gravity	rotate	temperature	enough
powerful	spectacular	measured	phenomena	massive

1 When we add endings to words (**suffixes**) we don't hear the suffix vowel sound very clearly and this can make them difficult to spell. Write the words from the list with the suffixes below, and then learn them using the **look–say–cover–write–check** method.

a -ous ______________________ b -ful ______________________

c -ar ______________________ d -ive ______________________

e -able ______________________ f -ure ______________________

2 Choose a word from the list to complete these sentences.

a If planet Earth did not ________________ on its axis, we would not have night and day.

b Earth is 149.6 ________________ kilometres from the Sun.

c A high-jumper on the Moon could jump over a house, because of the weak ____________.

d There is a big ________________ between the night sky of the Northern Hemisphere and that of the Southern Hemisphere.

e Astronauts would ________________ and die if they took off their space suits.

3 ***Sphere*** and ***phenomena*** have a ***ph*** spelling for a "f" sound. (***Phenomena*** is the plural of ***phenomenon***.) Can you match these ***ph*** words to their meanings? Use a dictionary if you need to.

a	phenomenon	solid round object or shape
b	phantom	someone who uses reason to understand humans and their world
c	phase	imaginary bird in ancient stories
d	philosopher	ghostly apparition
e	phoenix	something interesting or unusual that has been observed
f	phony	short group of words
g	prophet	stage in a process
h	phrase	prize or award
i	sphere	someone who predicts the future
j	trophy	fake, unreal

4 An astronomer is a scientist who studies the universe and space. Can you fill in the missing letters to make other kinds of scientists?

a B ___ ___ ___ ___ IST: a scientist who studies plants

b B ___ ___ ___ O ___ IST: a scientist who studies living things

c ___ E ___ L ___ ___ IST: a scientist who studies rocks and the Earth's structure

d ___ ___ Y ___ ICIST: a scientist who studies natural laws of physical matter and energy

e C ___ ___ ___ IST: a scientist who studies chemical reactions

Grammar—Singular and plural agreement

Look at these sentences:
A star <u>starts</u> out as a cloud of hydrogen gas and dust. ✓
A star <u>start</u> out as a cloud of hydrogen gas and dust. ✗
Stars <u>are</u> huge balls of flaming gas. ✓
Stars <u>is</u> huge balls of flaming gas. ✗
If the subject is **singular**, you need a **singular verb**. If the subject is **plural**, you need a **plural verb**.
The subject and verb must agree.

Now look at how these sentences continue, using pronouns instead of the noun subjects.
The pronouns are shown in *italics*.
A star <u>starts</u> out as a cloud of hydrogen gas and dust. *It* <u>begins</u> to form. As *it* collapses, *it* <u>begins</u> to rotate and heat up. ✓
Stars <u>are</u> huge balls of flaming gas. *They* <u>are</u> like huge nuclear furnaces. *They* <u>throw</u> out enormous quantities of light, heat and other forms of energy. ✓
Always check that your subjects and verbs **agree in singular or plural**. Also check that the **pronouns** used to refer back to the subjects **agree**.

Correct the singular/plural agreement where needed in these sentences. The first one has been done for you.

a Comets are frozen lifeless bodies. ~~It~~ *They* only ~~comes~~ *come* to life when near the Sun's heat.

b Meteors are sometimes called 'shooting stars' but it is not really a star.

c Some meteors are coloured, mostly blue and white, though it might sometimes be red or green.

d A communication satellite bounce signals from one point on Earth to another point.

e Galaxies are vast clusters of thousands of millions of stars. It is classified according to its shape.

f Telescopes magnify distant objects in the night sky. It uses lenses and mirrors to make things appear closer and larger.

DID YOU KNOW?
There is a word to describe numbers with a million zeros!
It is 'googol'.

Punctuation—Brackets

We use **brackets to include extra bits of information**, especially definitions and measurements.
Look at these examples from "Stars":
… but this is only because it is the closest (about 150 million kilometres away) …
… is 4.3 light years away. (One light year is the distance that light travels in one year.)

Can you add the extra bits of information from the box to the sentences below, enclosing them in brackets?

146 million kilometres away	opposite to Earth	around 465 degrees Celsius
named after the Roman goddess of love	only 652 kilometres less in diameter	

a The earth is the third planet from the Sun ______________________________.

b Venus ______________________________ is Earth's closest neighbour.

c Venus is also the closest in size to Earth ______________________________.

d Venus spins from west to east ______________________________.

e Venus is the hottest planet in the solar system ______________________________.

Can you help?

Can you fix up these mistakes with singular and plural agreement? The wriggly lines will help you.

People used to think comets were fireballs but that is not correct. It is actually a frozen, lifeless body most of the time. They have solid centres of dirty ice surrounded by gas. It only comes to life when it comes near the Sun, because the Sun heats them up and releases gases trapped inside. These gases are what forms the tails of comets. The tails of comets can be millions of kilometres long—it is really only because of its tail that we see comets at all. Comets orbit the Sun just like planets but its orbit are far greater and so it lasts much longer. Some take thousands of years to complete their orbit. The most famous comet is Halley's comet, which comes round about every 76 years. The last time was in 1986, and it is expected to return in 2061.

Puzzle time

1 Can you unscramble these SPACE words?

a SARM __ __ __ __

b CTMEO __ __ __ __ __

c STAROTAUN __ [ ] __ __ __ __ __ __ __

d REJPUIT __ __ __ [ ] __ __ __

e MTEEOTIRE __ [ ] __ __ __ __ __ __ __

f NEVSU [ ] __ __ __ __

g TASRUN __ __ __ __ __ __

h USURAN [ ] __ __ __ __ __

i TUNEPEN [ ] __ __ __ __ __

j CERMRYU __ __ [ ] __ __ __ __

k RATHE ☐ ___ ___ ___ ___

l XAGLYA ___ ___ ___ ___ ___ ___

m TLPUO ___ ___ ___ ___ ___

2 Now write the letters from the boxes in activity 1 and unscramble them to get a word that covers them all! ___ ___ ___ ___ ___ ___ ___ ___ → ______________________

3 Can you unscramble the letters below to make a word meaning people with this job?

MOON STARERS → ______________________________

Your turn to write

Tips for marvellously meteoric writers

You usually write reports after reading or watching something, so you'll often have more information than you need.

Don't try to include everything—just select the most important and interesting facts.

Also, don't just copy an information text—use your own words.

Then make a plan—organise your facts under headings before you start your draft.

1 Here are some facts about galaxies. Use the information to draft a report on the topic in the space on the next page. The headings will help you organise your information.

- Change the order of the information around if you think you need to.
- Use your own words where possible.
- Leave out any information you do not understand.
- Explain anything the reader might not understand—you could get definitions of ***light year*** and ***black hole*** from the "Stars" text.

Galaxies

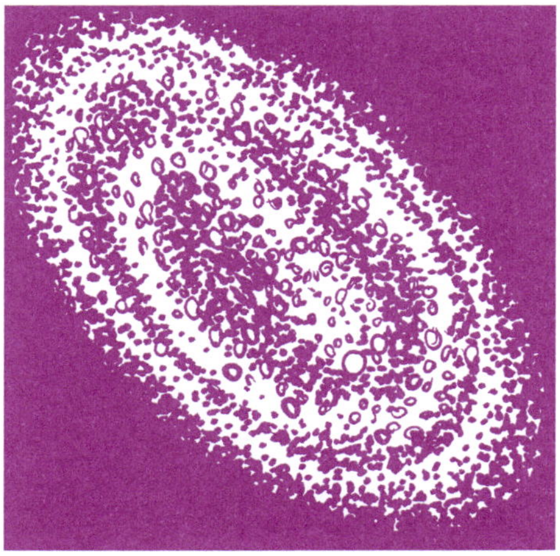

- vast clusters of thousands of millions of stars, planets, gases and dust
- like islands in an ocean of space
- held together by gravity
- 1000 million galaxies
- every galaxy a very long way from all others
- formed during Big Bang explosion about 15 000 million years ago
- formed from lumps of matter that resulted from Big Bang explosion
- classified according to shapes
- most common type is spiral—like a catherine-wheel firework—but some oval, some irregular
- our galaxy—the Milky Way—spiral shaped
- our solar system on edge of galaxy
- contains about 100 billion stars—still producing new ones
- about 100 000 light years across
- astronomers think an enormous black hole is at centre of our galaxy
- although Milky Way is massive, is only small part of Universe—one of millions of similar galaxies

What are galaxies?

How were they formed?

What do they look like?

Our own galaxy: the Milky Way

2. Write a report on another topic related to space and the universe (e.g. planets, comets, meteorites, the Moon, the Sun, space travel, galaxies, black holes, the Milky Way or one particular planet). Look through some books first to find a topic that really interests you. Then follow the steps below to write an information report on your topic. Use the space below for your notes or a first draft, and then write your report in your Writer's Notebook.
   - Do some research to find out some facts about your topic.
   - Decide what you want to include in your report (you can't include everything).
   - Organise your facts into three or four sub-topics.
   - Begin your draft report with a definition of your topic.
   - Draft your sub-topic paragraphs.
   - Revise your draft and check your spelling, punctuation and grammar. Look out especially for singular/plural agreement. Look out too that you have kept your report factual, and have not included your own opinions.

Chapter 7 Writing a description

The aim of a description is to give your reader a clear and vivid picture of a person, thing, place or scene. It is often part of a longer text such as a narrative. This text is a description of a scene.

STRUCTURE

LANGUAGE

This description is from a novel written as the diary of a young English boy called David Bellamy. It is 1807 and David has been sent to live in Sydney Town with his uncle and aunt after his parents have died. He has travelled as a passenger on a convict ship. The extract describes the scene at the docks a day after his ship has landed, and the convicts are starting to come off the ship. He is waiting outside a building where he is to meet his uncle.

Thursday 17th December

I am writing this while I sit in front of the building and already I am receiving strange glances. A soldier sitting on a pile of ropes studied me as I sat down and undid the lid of my ink. He seemed satisfied and promptly took a swig from his bottle, closed his eyes and is now sleeping. Each person who wanders past me, stares. There is a woman just now, with a baby wrapped in a shawl, and she calls to another to come and see what I am doing. I ignore them. A boy about my age is fishing at the edge. He has just caught a large silver fish and he flicked it up high in the air. It landed beside him and flopped about as he tried to take the hook from its mouth. Blood splashed on his hands. Even now, in the bag behind him, I see squirming and imagine that fish gasping for its last breath of air.

The convicts are coming off. They are strangely quiet now, staring at the wide expanse of sky, not seen by them since we crossed the Line some months back. Perhaps, like me, they cannot believe how blue this sky can be and how harsh is the Southern sun. But I have grown used to it these past days. I know a splash of water on my skin or clothes will dry in moments. They are pitiful in their rags. They stagger forth and many stumble and fall, clutching at their fellows when they reach solid land. It is as if the Earth still moves under foot, so accustomed are we to the movements of the ocean waves. Soldiers are everywhere, easy to see in their bright red jackets although some are torn and, in places, more brown than red. They stamp up and down the length of the area, shouting at the convicts and pushing those who move too slowly or who step away from the line. I cannot hear clearly the words the soldiers say but their tone is rough and angry. A convict boy, no bigger than myself, catches my eye and says something, which I also cannot hear. He thrusts his arm forward in a wild gesture and twists his face so I know his words are unkind. What can he have done to be sent to this place? The wretches are marched off, away from where I sit. I am hungry. I wish my Uncle would come.

From *My Story: The Rum Rebellion: The Diary of David Bellamy*, by Libby Gleeson, 2001.

Orientation to topic: who, what, when, where

Description of the scene: physical things (objects, buildings, landscape); actions and behaviours; sounds; atmosphere

Paragraphs to separate different parts of scene, or different time periods

Concluding comment (not always necessary)

Common nouns to name people or things

Phrases and clauses to add detail

Interesting, expressive verbs

Language that creates clear pictures of people and things

Usually ***present tense verbs***

Descriptive adjectives

What did you read?

1. In paragraph 1, what is the soldier doing? ______________________

   What is the boy doing? ______________________

2. In paragraph 2, which two groups of people are described? ______________________

   What are they doing? ______________________

   ____

3. Sometimes a writer does not give you all the information. You have to work it out yourself. Answer these questions based on the information in the text.

   a Why do people stare at David and give him strange glances (what is he doing that might be unusual)? ______________________

   b Why is David more used to the sky and sun than the convicts are? ______________________

   ____

   c What do you think 'the Line' is? ______________________

   d Why do the convicts find it difficult to walk? ______________________

   ____

   e Why is the young convict boy angry with David? ______________________

   ____

4. The atmosphere is different in the two paragraphs.

   a Which paragraph suggests a dark, rather gloomy atmosphere? ____________

   b Which paragraph suggests a bright, calm atmosphere? ____________

How was it written?

1. David does not describe every single thing or person he sees. Instead he describes the most I __ __ __ __ __ __ __ __ __ __ things and people. In paragraph 1, for example, he only describes __ __ __ __ __ people.

2. David gives a sense of the sounds as well as the sights of the scene.

   a What words tell us about the sound of the convicts? ______________________

   b What words tell us about the sound of the soldiers? ______________________

3. David chooses good verbs to show the action. Write two verbs used to describe:

   a what the fish does. ______________________

   b the way the convicts move. ______________________

   c the way the soldiers behave. ______________________

   d the gestures of the young convict boy. ______________________

4. a Do you have a clear image of the scene after reading the description? (yes/no) ____________

   b Draw a picture of the scene on your own paper.

Spelling and meaning

glances	soldier	promptly	swig	wanders
wrapped	pitiful	stagger	stumble	clutching
although	rough	thrusts	gesture	wretches

1 Use a word from the word box in these sentences, then learn them using the **look–say–cover–write–check** method.

a The poor ________________ had spent six whole months on board ship.

b The woman stares at me and then ________________ a book roughly into my face.

c The man got his meaning across using only facial expressions and a hand ________________.

d It was ________________ to see how thin and pale the convicts were.

e The old man ________________ aimlessly around the street ________________ a tiny leather bag to his chest.

f The sick and injured ________________ and ________________ as they are pushed along.

g The ________________ was very ________________ with the convicts.

h ________________ she was ________________ in a shawl, she was shivering with the cold.

i He had a ________________ of rum and then ________________ fell down at my feet.

2 There are many vivid verbs in the English language to describe the way people walk or move. Here are some from the text:

stagger stumble stamp march squirm flop twist

Here are a few more:

dash shuffle stomp flit glide prowl pace tramp slip totter lumber hobble scurry slither

Can you match any of the verbs above to the person or animal below? Use your dictionary to help you. (You might find more than one verb for each.)

a A very, very old person: ________________

b A dancer on stage: ________________

c A person waiting to hear important news: ________________

d A person in a hurry: ________________

e A huge ogre or monster: ________________

f A skater or acrobat: ________________

g An animal waiting to catch prey: ________________

h A person with an injury: ________________

i A person on stilts or high heels: ________________

j A mouse: ________________

k A snake or lizard: ________________

3 ***Thrust*** and ***clutch*** are good verbs to describe the way people move their hands. Look up these other "hand movement" verbs in your dictionary.

grasp	pluck	wrench	seize	grapple	clasp	jostle	cradle	heave

Grammar—Adjectival and adverbial phrases

We sometimes want to give our readers a clearer picture about the people and things (the **nouns**) we write about—**whose, with what, where, what like, about what, what kind, why.**

Examples A boy <u>about my age</u> is fishing …
They are pitiful <u>in their rags</u>.
There is a woman just now, <u>with a baby wrapped in a shawl</u>.

Phrases that add information to nouns are called **adjectival phrases**.

At other times we want to give our readers a clearer picture about what the people and things are doing (the **verbs**)—**when, where, how, why**.

Examples A soldier sitting <u>on a pile of ropes</u> studied me
He thrusts his arm forward <u>in a wild gesture</u> …

Phrases that add information to verbs are called **adverbial phrases**.

All the phrases above begin with **prepositions**—such as ***on***, ***in***, ***with***, ***without***, ***about***, ***up***, ***at***, ***across***, ***from***, ***to***, ***beside***, ***next to***, ***like***, ***for***—but not all phrases do.

1 Underline the phrases in these sentences and circle the prepositions.

a Their hair is knotted with dirt and straw.

b The trip across the oceans was harsh and long.

c Many of the women by the docks were carrying small children.

d Children played quite happily on the pebbly shore.

e I felt sick with grief and loneliness.

f Travellers led their weary horses to the water troughs outside the public house. (two phrases)

2 Add phrases to these sentences to give more information about the underlined nouns or verbs. Use the prepositions in brackets.

a The old man wore a <u>coat</u> (with) ______________________________

b I could see a long <u>line of children</u> (outside) ______________________________

c The animals <u>were</u> hungry and thirsty (after) ______________________________

d The trees provided no real <u>protection</u> (from) ______________________________

e The sky <u>was</u> heavy (with) ______________________________

f The prisoners <u>looked</u> longingly (at) ______________________________

Punctuation—Commas to add descriptive detail

We often need a **comma before and after a descriptive detail** to make our meaning clear, especially when the detail comes in the middle of a sentence.

Examples There is a woman just now, with a baby wrapped in a shawl, and she calls to another …
A convict boy, no bigger than myself, catches my eye …

However, we don't always need a comma. For example, we don't need one when the detail identifies the person or thing.
Example A soldier sitting on a pile of ropes studied me as I sat down …
In this sentence, we are identifying which soldier we are talking about—that is, the one sitting on the pile of ropes.
The best way to know if a comma is needed is to read the sentence out loud with commas and without commas, and see which sounds better.

Put commas where needed in these sentences. Remember: read them out loud with and without commas.

a The boys hoping to reach the top by sundown pushed on in the fading light.

b A small girl hat tucked under her arm smiled shyly at us.

c There are ten men in the room all sitting around a small table and they look up as we enter.

d My uncle usually a rough-spoken man gently asked the boy his name.

e The swimmers exhausted by their adventure flung themselves onto the riverbank.

f The students playing near the basketball nets are in trouble.

g The small children kept awake by the noise huddled together under the blankets.

h The old man his eyes flashing angrily refused to move.

i The boy looking this way is the thief.

Can you help?

This student wrote a description of a parade in a letter to her friend while on holidays. However, she forgot to use any punctuation and spelt some words wrongly. Can you correct her writing?

I am siting here in a café in the town square wating for a parade to begin althogh the day is extremly cold the crowd is huge everone is very exited and very noisy as they wait for the parade to start I can here trumpets and drums the parade has begun leading the parade are peple on stilts waring bright-coloured hats and floing capes one stumbels for a second before steadying up and continuing on the croud cheers the stilt-walkers are folowed by some very small childern their faces are painted with animel masks and they are cluching balloons in their hands now I can see young grils in bodysuits doing cartweels and tumbles the sene changes every minute each time a new group appears the crowd shouts out and cheers wildly the biggest cheer is given to the town band at the end of the parade and to a little boy playing a very big drum.

Puzzle time

Can you unscramble the words on page 55? You'll find each one in the scene pictured.

a GGGBEAA ______________________

b TYTJE ______________________

c ROPRET ______________________

d DCKE ______________________

e GGNAYAW ______________________

f PSSGAENRE ______________________

g CHRONA ______________________

h SMAT ______________________

i RTHLOEOP ______________________

j CTPAIAN ______________________

Your turn to write

Tip for dynamically descriptive writers

When you describe a scene, don't include every single thing you can see. Describe only the things that are interesting or that you can describe in an interesting way. Give detail about these things to make the scene come alive.

1 Let's try writing a short description of a familiar scene that involves a few people.
If you are at home, go and find somewhere where you can sit comfortably and observe people (members of your family, neighbours, passers-by) going about their everyday activities. You might go to the kitchen, the lounge-room, the balcony, the backyard or the front porch, for example.
If you are at school, stay in the classroom or go somewhere in the playground.

a Now imagine you are describing the scene for someone who has never seen it and knows nothing about it—perhaps as part of a diary or a letter. Take a few minutes to look around you. Think about these points, and then jot down your ideas around the questions.

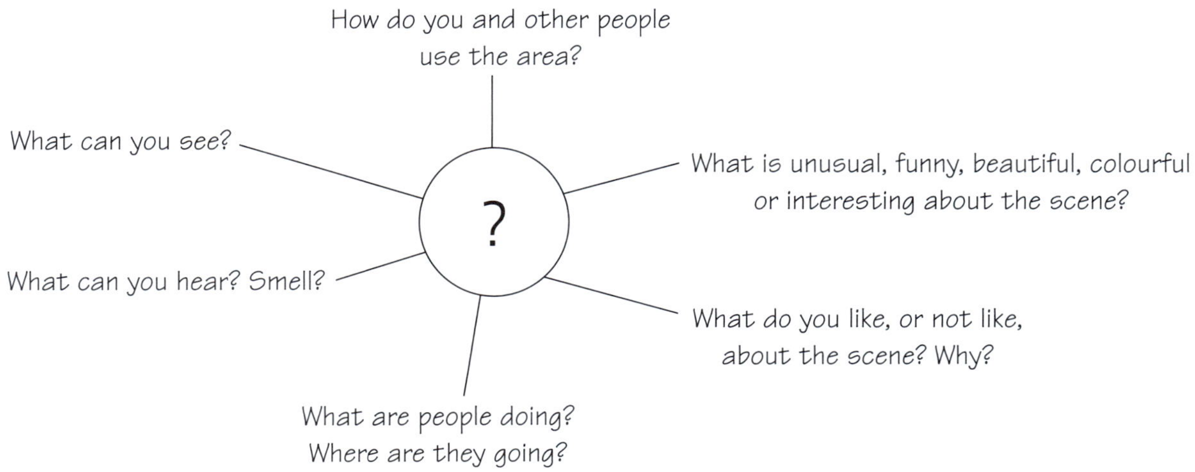

b Now you should be ready to write a draft of your description below, using your notes. You could begin as David Bellamy did: "I am writing this while I sit …" If you wish, revise your draft and write it in your Writer's Notebook.

2 Now write a description of any scene you like that has special importance for you. If you are not near the scene at the moment, you will have to depend on your imagination, and your memories. Here are some suggestions:

- a place where you go for holidays (e.g. a farm, a river, a beach, the mountains, a camping site)
- a new place you have moved to (a house, a street, a town, a country)
- the home of a friend or family member (e.g. your cousins' place, your grandparents' place)
- a busy railway station, bus station or airport
- a wharf where boats of some kind come in (e.g. fishing boats, ocean liners)

Again, imagine you are writing your description as part of a diary or letter to be read by someone far away, who knows nothing about the scene you are describing. Think about what they would find interesting.

Brainstorm ideas as you did in activity 1 before you start writing. Remember that you don't have to describe everything—just the most interesting things about the scene. Write your description in your Writer's Notebook.

DID YOU KNOW?

Children as young as eight or nine years of age were sometimes transported to Australia in the late 1700s and early 1800s for small crimes. Most were orphans who had had to make their own way in the world from a very early age. *Oliver Twist*, by Charles Dickens, tells of young people in this situation.

Answers on pages 96–97

Chapter 8 Giving an opinion speech (exposition)

When you give an opinion speech, your aim is to persuade your audience that your opinion is right and sensible. Because you want your audience to listen closely to what you are saying, you should also try to make it interesting and entertaining. An opinion speech is a kind of exposition.

STRUCTURE | LANGUAGE

Zoos are cruel places. Do you agree?

Good morning 6K. Last August, I visited Melbourne Zoo and saw a baby Sumatran Orangutan. His birth was part of an international program to help the Sumatran Orangutan survive as a species. At the moment these beautiful creatures are in danger of disappearing in the next 10 to 20 years.

Melbourne Zoo is a modern zoo. Like most modern zoos, it cares very much about animals. It is NOT a cruel place. You could certainly argue that zoos WERE cruel places in the past, but I don't believe you can argue that they ARE cruel places today.

In the past, zoos were exhibition parks. Their only purpose was to give humans pleasure, by showing them wonderful, exotic creatures that they would otherwise never see. Because animals were only there for the benefit of humans like you and me, no one took much care of them. They were transported thousands of miles around the world, then locked up in small, bare, lonely cages. In those days, zoos were cruel.

These days, things are very different. The whole purpose of zoos has changed. Now zoos have three major purposes: education, conservation and research. They aim to make animals better off everywhere. Because of this, the way animals are cared for is also different.

Firstly, education. Education is a big part of the activity at zoos. At Sydney's Taronga Park Zoo, for example, 130,000 school children attend special programs every year to learn about how animals behave and what they need to live. The aim is to make children more aware of animals now so that they will care about them when they are adults. It is the same in most zoos all around the world.

Secondly, conservation. Zoos play a major role in the protection and conservation of endangered species. The Sumatran Orangutan is just one example of the many animals that are better off because of special breeding programs. Perhaps you have been to the Western Plains Zoo in Dubbo and learnt about the Black Rhinoceros breeding program? Or maybe you have even seen new babies like I did?

Lastly, research. Zoos are involved in many important research programs which help animals in captivity and in the wild. Recent research, for example, has shown that many intelligent animals benefit from being given puzzles to solve while in captivity, so now many zoos are providing mental challenges in their monkey enclosures.

Modern zoos care about animals first, and people second. The people who work in them care about the animals' comfort, their freedom and their survival as species. Zoos ARE NOT cruel places. Thank you for listening.

Maria Masri

Structure:

Greeting to audience

Introduction to topic and your point of view

Something to ***capture the audience's interest***

Series of arguments given one at a time

Arguments developed with one or two examples or details

Conclusion repeats point of view and rounds off the talk

Thanks to audience for listening

Language:

Talking about your ***own experience***

Capitals or highlighting to remind speaker to emphasise words

Talking directly to audience to make it more personal

Opinion adjectives

Interesting detail

Connectives to show that you are moving to a new point

Questions to involve the audience

Sentences not too long and complicated

What did you read?

1. Does Maria agree or disagree with the statement that zoos are cruel? ______________________

2. Complete the sentences. According to Maria:
   a Zoos of the past put ______________ first, but modern zoos put ________________ first.
   b The purpose of zoos of the past was ____
   ____
   c The three main purposes of modern zoos are ____
   ____

3. Circle the best answer. Zoos put on programs for children to:
   a show them animals adults don't usually see.
   b make them care about animals when they are adults.
   c teach them how animals behave.

4. Name one animal species mentioned that has been helped by special breeding programs recently.
   ____

How was it written?

1. In the first draft of her speech, Maria wrote the paragraph below as her first paragraph. Why do you think she changed it? ____

This morning I will talk about the difference between the past and the present. I will talk about the purpose of zoos today—education, conservation and research—and how this has made them places where animals are very well treated.

2. Circle the best answer. The main argument that ties all the smaller arguments together is:
   a Zoos of the past were cruel but zoos today are not.
   b Zoos aim to educate people about animals.
   c The main purposes of zoos are research, education and conservation.

3. Maria organised her arguments and spoke about them one at a time. Can you put the arguments she covered in the order she mentions them? (Write 1, 2, 3, 4 or 5.)

   Zoos and research _____ Purpose of zoos today _____
   Zoos and education _____ Purpose of zoos in the past _____
   Zoos and conservation _____

4. Using ***you***, ***I***, ***we*** and asking your audience questions are two ways to make your speech more personal and get your audience to listen. Look back at the speech and underline all the times Maria uses ***you***. How many did you find? __________

5. How convincing do you find the arguments in the speech? (Tick one)

   Very convincing _____ Quite convincing _____
   Not very convincing _____ Not at all convincing _____
   Give your reasons. ____
   ____

Spelling and meaning

international	survives	species	disappearing	modern
cruel	certainly	believe	purpose	pleasure
protection	conservation	research	endangered	captivity

Tip for spectacular spellers
Long words look hard but are often easier to spell than short ones because they are spelt the way they sound. Breaking words up into syllables helps to avoid missing out letters (e.g. ***con-serv-a-tion***).

1 Slowly say the word box words out loud, breaking them into syllables. (The important thing is to have one vowel sound in each syllable.) Write the words that have:

a one syllable ______

b two syllables ______

______

c three syllables ______

d four syllables ______

e the most syllables ______ How many syllables does this word have? ____

2 In the words ***certainly*** and ***species*** the letter ***c*** is used for the ***s*** sound. This is called a 'soft ***c***'. Choose one of the 'soft ***c***' words from the box below to fill each gap.

science	recently	century	centre	exceptions	excellent	celebrated

a In the 19th ______, animals in zoos were poorly treated.

b Research is very important in ______.

c Most modern zoos provide ______ care for the animals, but there are ______.

d ______ Adelaide Zoo ______ the birth of a baby zebra.

3 Can you draw lines between the matching synonyms below?

pleasure vanish disappear aim benefit recent display endangered

merciless advantage cruel research exhibition certainly

satisfaction purpose study modern definitely threatened

4 Choose a word from the word box to fill each gap.

a An ______ species is one that is in danger of becoming extinct in the next ten to twenty years.

b You have to ______ the topic to prepare a good speech.

c Breeding in ______ can help species to survive.

d Poachers who kill for profit are one of the main dangers for many ______.

e Do you ______ that zoos care mostly about the animals?

f The program was ______, linking Australia with many countries around the world.

Grammar—Connectives

Connectives are words that **show how your ideas are connected** from one sentence or paragraph to another. They are very important when you give an opinion in a speech or in writing.
In the speech about zoos, for example, the connectives ***firstly***, ***secondly*** and ***lastly*** showed that the speaker was listing a series of points—moving from one point to another. The connectives ***in the past*** and ***these days*** showed that she was contrasting two different time periods.
Look at these different kinds of connectives.

Listing a series of points	**Adding new or extra information**	**Giving examples**	**Talking about different time periods**	**Contrasting ideas**	**Showing causes and results**
first of all to start with next firstly secondly finally	also furthermore besides as well	for example for instance	then now in the past these days at the moment	however on the other hand in contrast nevertheless	so as a result therefore because of this

Write the connectives below in the right space to show the connection between ideas in these sentences.

as a result	firstly	for example	however	nevertheless	secondly

a Most zoos these days take very good care of the animals. ______________________, it was not always this way.

b Many breeding programs have been a great success. The White Rhino, ______________________, was nearly extinct in the 1960s but is now back at safe levels.

c A breeding program for the Bald Eagle has been in place for the last few decades. ______________________, the Bald Eagle has recovered to numbers of 50 years ago.

d Since 1984 in Zimbabwe, rangers have worked hard to stop poachers killing Black Rhinos. ______________________, in that time, more than 1170 rhinos have been killed.

e I believe that zoos are cruel places. ________________, animals must put up with human beings all day. ______________, there is absolutely no need for animals to be there.

Punctuation—Highlighting

When you write out your speech, it is a good idea to **highlight** some words (by underlining or writing in capital letters). This will remind you which words to **emphasise or say with special expression**. The best way to find out which words to highlight is to read your speech out loud beforehand.
Full stops, commas, exclamation marks and question marks also help you deliver a speech well. For example, they tell you when to pause, when to look up at your audience, and when to change your voice in some way.

1. Read out loud the paragraph from the zoo speech below, emphasising the words in capitals.

   Melbourne Zoo is a modern zoo. Like most modern zoos it cares very much about animals. It is NOT a cruel place. You could certainly argue that zoos WERE cruel places in the past, but I don't believe you can argue that they ARE cruel places today.

   Did you notice how emphasising these words helps to make clear the contrast between the past and the present?

2. Now read out loud these paragraphs from the zoo speech, and underline the words you would emphasise to get the main point across (only three or four in each paragraph).

   In the past, zoos were exhibition parks. Their only purpose was to give humans pleasure, by showing them wonderful, exotic creatures that they would otherwise never see. Because animals were only there for the benefit of humans like you and me, no one took much care of them. They were transported thousands of miles around the world, then locked up in small, bare, lonely cages. In those days, zoos were cruel.

   These days, things are very different. The whole purpose of zoos has changed. Now zoos have three major purposes: education, conservation and research. They aim to make animals better off everywhere. Because of this, the way animals are cared for is also different.

Can you help?

This student wrote this paragraph for a speech arguing against killing animals for fur. Can you put the sentences into the order that makes the argument make sense? Use the connectives and other words in *italics* to help you.

a ______ *They* buy them to look beautiful.

b ______ Of course, *the people* who buy animal furs and skins *nowadays* don't buy them to keep warm and dry.

c 1__ Killing animals to make clothing is completely unnecessary *in this day and age*.

d ______ *They* did not have the technology we have *these days* to keep ourselves warm and dry using other materials like cotton and synthetics.

e ______ I wonder if *they* think about the poor animals killed in the process.

f ______ *In the Stone Age, humans* had to kill animals for their fur and skin, because that was the only way they could survive.

DID YOU KNOW?
There are about 1000 endangered species in the world today.

Puzzle time

How many of these zoo words can you find in the wordsearch?

zoo conservation parks protected endangered species habitat vulnerable wildlife poaching threat breeding nature extinct hunting control population research

R	B	P	E	Q	B	W	R	E	T	R	J	I	K	H	C	Z	I	O	P	L	F	S
F	W	U	R	H	A	B	I	T	A	T	T	V	H	G	F	E	Q	E	A	I	B	M
U	R	E	I	N	M	L	D	L	R	E	W	N	U	O	T	Y	B	V	E	H	Y	U
E	N	D	A	N	G	E	R	E	D	X	S	D	F	L	A	I	T	B	N	Y	I	L
I	L	B	P	S	R	P	O	P	U	L	A	T	I	O	N	R	T	Y	B	V	E	W
P	U	Y	G	S	Z	X	I	O	L	F	I	T	Y	U	R	E	S	E	A	R	C	H
P	R	C	M	O	A	L	B	C	E	W	R	F	F	A	S	L	R	B	F	E	O	U
A	O	X	N	G	R	P	R	O	T	E	C	T	E	D	U	T	R	A	T	H	W	R
R	Q	A	E	L	O	Q	E	N	T	Y	O	D	S	A	G	B	K	G	B	T	M	O
K	W	R	C	T	K	I	E	T	R	T	N	T	Y	N	I	A	Q	M	N	L	D	B
S	Y	T	R	H	L	Y	D	R	T	Y	S	P	E	C	I	E	S	T	R	S	E	T
Q	U	U	T	R	I	Z	I	O	R	E	E	T	Y	F	F	X	S	D	X	K	L	I
L	P	I	O	E	Y	N	N	L	R	F	R	D	G	H	J	T	L	J	H	A	P	K
O	K	P	G	A	Q	A	G	R	T	A	V	A	T	S	G	I	T	Y	U	B	V	F
R	S	O	F	T	W	F	M	E	G	P	A	R	F	H	U	N	T	I	N	G	K	J
T	A	A	S	U	D	D	G	W	Z	G	T	H	K	G	O	C	Q	W	E	T	H	F
B	E	C	D	Y	G	H	F	Q	F	O	I	T	J	F	I	T	A	L	H	P	R	O
V	F	O	Y	Q	M	T	S	P	S	G	O	E	Q	A	E	M	L	T	G	I	R	E
W	G	L	F	P	B	L	A	M	K	D	N	A	T	U	R	E	P	E	Q	T	U	A

Your turn to write

Tips for seriously sophisticated speakers

It is not just how you write your speech that is important, it is how you deliver it to your audience. Here are some tips to help you:

- Write your speech on small cards.
- Look up from your cards as much as you can.
- Make eye contact with different people in the audience.
- Pause often to give your audience time to catch up. It is a good idea to write STOP! in big letters on your cards after every few lines.
- Speak loudly and clearly. Imagine you are speaking to the person at the back of the room.
- Try not to be nervous. Smile at your audience. They will usually smile back and you will immediately feel better.

1 Here are three points you could make in a speech to show that zoos are not cruel. Develop the points by giving an example (perhaps from your own experience of visiting zoos).

a Zoos these days do everything possible to make animals feel at home.

____

____

____

b Zoos these days do everything possible to keep animals in good health.

____

____

____

c More and more zoos are allowing the animals to roam free and enclosing the human visitors instead.

2 There is always more than one way to look at a topic, and it is a good idea to think of both sides when preparing a speech. In a debate you are told which side of an argument you have to take and it might not be the side you really agree with!
Imagine you were told to argue that zoos ARE cruel places. Read the points below and choose *three only* to use in a speech. Write your speech in the space below.

- Zoos take animals out of the natural web of life.
- Exposing animals to humans all the time has negative effects.
- The trapping of animals sometimes hurts or even kills animals.
- Animals in zoos are there for the entertainment of humans.
- Keeping animals in zoos is unnatural.
- There are still many zoos around the world that keep animals enclosed in small spaces.
- We don't need zoos to educate us. We can watch wildlife programs.
- We have no way of knowing what animals feel.
- Most animal species in zoos are not endangered.
- Research can be done in the wild.

Introduction (Try to catch the audience's interest immediately. State the topic and your point of view.)

First argument (Show audience you are moving to your first argument, state your argument and develop it with an example.)

Second argument (Show them you are moving on to your second point, state the argument and develop it with an example.)

Third argument (Show them you are moving on to your third point, state your argument and develop it with an example.)

Conclusion (Repeat your view and round off your talk.)

3 Choose one of the topics below. Write a two-minute speech giving your opinion for or against. (Use your Writer's Notebook.)

- We should not keep pets.
- We should not kill animals for their fur or skins.
- Cats are an environmental pest and should be outlawed.
- It is always worth saving animals from extinction.

Answers on pages 97–98

Chapter 9 Writing an explanation

The aim of an explanation is to tell how or why something happens. Explanations are often about natural or scientific phenomena, processes or events.

STRUCTURE

LANGUAGE

What causes a tsunami?

1. Tsunamis are freakishly large waves which are usually formed when the seabed is disturbed by an underwater earthquake or by a volcano. They can also be caused by hurricanes or underwater landslides.

2. When tsunamis are out at sea, they may be only one metre high, but they travel at great speeds —up to 600 kilometres an hour. As they come into shore, the sea gets shallower, which slows the wave down and lets all the water behind it catch up. This then makes the wave grow larger and larger. Tsunamis sometimes even form up to 40 metres high and go three kilometres inland.

3. A tsunami is usually very destructive. It crashes down everything in its path and then sucks it all out to sea—even humans and livestock. Some tsunamis have killed tens of thousands of people at a time. For example, the massive tsunami across the Indian Ocean in December 2004 claimed more than 280 000 lives. Tsunamis are one of the most deadly natural disasters.

Patrick Thomas

Structure:
- ***Statement identifying the phenomenon*** —often a definition or classification
- ***Explanation of the phenomenon***—how or why it occurs
- ***Additional information*** about the phenomenon

Language:
- Mainly ***factual information***
- ***Words to express cause and effect***
- ***Time words***
- ***Name*** of the phenomenon is ***often the first words*** of sentences

What causes an earthquake?

1. Earthquakes are one of the most powerful of the natural forces on our planet, but what are they and what sets them off?

2. An earthquake is when there is a trembling or vibration (a 'quake') of the earth's surface. It occurs where there is a 'fault' or break in the earth's crust. The blocks on either side of the fault move up and down against each other, or shift lengthways. The friction that results produces a lot of energy. This energy is changed to vibration in the rocks, and we feel this vibration as an earthquake. The ground starts to feel like the deck of a ship and then starts to completely break up, or rise or fall. Buildings fall down, bridges tumble and dams burst.

3. Earthquakes are happening all the time but most are tremors that are only noticed by seismologists who study them. Every few years there is a really catastrophic one which leads to the death of thousands of people. The last major earthquake was in Iran in 2003, when 8000 people were killed.

4. Although we know much more about earthquakes nowadays, we can probably never prevent them. The best thing we can do is stop people living in earthquake areas and make sure buildings are earthquake proof.

Kenny Chew

Structure:
- ***Statement identifying the phenomenon*** —often a definition or classification
- ***Explanation of the phenomenon***—how or why it occurs
- ***Additional information*** about the phenomenon
- ***Concluding comment*** (not always)

Language:
- ***Technical words***, often with everyday explanations
- Some ***passive voice***
- Usually ***present tense verbs***
- ***Many compound and complex sentences***

What did you read?

1. What four natural events can cause tsunamis? ________________

____

2. True or false?

   a Tsunamis travel faster near the land. ________________

   b Tsunamis are bigger near the land. ________________

   c As the wave slows down it gets bigger. ________________

3. What is a 'fault'? ________________________________

4. Do you think tremors are small or large earthquakes? ________________

5. Circle the best answer. Which of these word sequences shows how earthquakes happen?

   a Movement → friction → energy → vibration

   b Friction → movement → vibration → energy

   c Movement → energy → friction → vibration

How was it written?

1. Explanations often include a definition of the phenomenon being explained. Underline the definition of ***tsunami*** in text 1 and ***earthquake*** in text 2.

2. In explanations you need to think about the best place to include your information.
   a Where would you add this sentence to the first text? (Put an X in the text.)
   Tsunamis have nothing at all to do with tides.
   b Where would you add these sentences to the second text? (Put an X in the text.)
      i Electricity lines are cut, gas and water mains are ruptured and fires break out, adding to the destruction.
      ii The worst earthquake last century was in north-east China at T'ang-shan in 1976 where 240 000 people were killed.

3. In explanations, we often begin sentences with the name of the phenomenon (e.g. ***Tsunamis***, ***A tsunami***, ***Some tsunamis***), or with pronouns to replace these words (e.g. ***They***, ***It***). This helps our readers keep track of our ideas.
   a Circle every time Patrick or Kenny use ***tsunami*** or ***earthquake*** at the beginning of their sentences.
   b Underline every time they use the pronouns ***it*** or ***they*** at the start of sentences.

4. Did you find these students' explanations easy to understand? (yes/no) __________

   Would it have helped to have a diagram of what happens? (yes/no) __________

5. Draw a simple diagram of one phenomenon to show what happens—a tsunami building up as it gets closer to shore, or an earthquake beginning beneath the earth's surface. Use your own paper.

DID YOU KNOW?

On average, about 13 000 earthquakes are located each year—about 35 a day. Many are not located because they occur in remote areas or are too small to be detected.

Spelling and meaning

disturbed	earthquake	volcano	caused	hurricanes
landslides	shallower	destructive	livestock	eruption
vibration	occurs	friction	tremors	catastrophic

1. Put the words from the word box into alphabetical order. Remember: look at the second, third and fourth letters (and so on) if the first letters are the same. (Learn those you are not sure of using the **look–say–cover–write–check** method.)

2. Fill in the blanks with words from the word box.

   a ______________ are the same as avalanches.

   b The floods ______________ terrible damage to the coastal towns.

   c The wild winds ______________ the animals.

   d The ______________ of the volcano was totally unexpected.

   e Australia has not had many earthquakes but it has had many earth ______________.

   f The ______________ between the two rocks creates energy.

3. Many adjectives to describe disasters are made from (or *derived* from) nouns (e.g. ***catastrophic*** is derived from ***catastrophe***). Fill in the blanks to make the adjectives below. Write the nouns they are derived from next to them.

   a DIS ___ ___ TR ___ ___ S ______________

   b TR ___ GI ___ ______________

   c DE ___ T ___ UC ___ IVE ______________

   d TE ___ ___ IB ___ ___ ______________

   e HO ___ ___ IF ___ C ______________

   f SH ___ ___ ___ ING ______________

   g D ___ V ___ ST ___ TING ______________

   h C ___ L ___ MITOUS ______________

4 The word ***tsunami*** comes from the Japanese language, ***tsu*** meaning "harbour" and ***nami*** meaning "wave". Do you know these other words of Japanese origin?

a Paper folding: O ___ ___ ___ ___ ___ I

b A wide sleeved gown: K ___ ___ ___ ___ O

c A method of fighting: K ___ ___ ___ ___ E

d Singing along to words and a video: K ___ ___ ___ ___ ___ E

Grammar—Active and passive voice

When writing, we can choose either the **active voice** or **passive voice** of verbs. Look at these sentences:

An underwater earthquake disturbs the seabed. (active voice)
The seabed is disturbed by an underwater earthquake. (passive voice)

The information in both sentences is the same but the **emphasis** or **focus** is different. In the first sentence, the emphasis is on the *underwater earthquake* and what it does (it disturbs something). In the second, the emphasis is on the *seabed* and what happens to it (it is disturbed by something).

We usually put the words we want our readers to focus on at the beginning of the sentence.
We use the **active voice** when we want the focus on **who or what is doing something**, and what it does (e.g. An underwater earthquake disturbs the seabed).
We use the **passive voice** when we want the focus on the **thing that something is done to** and/or what is done to it (e.g. The seabed is disturbed by an underwater earthquake).
We also use the passive voice when it is not important to say who or what is doing something.
Example Sometimes survivors are found days after the earthquake occurs. (We're interested in the *survivors*, not who found them.)

All the sentences below are in the active voice. Can you change them so that they are in the passive voice? Begin with the underlined words.

a Earthquakes usually disrupt road and rail transport.
Answer: Road and rail transport are usually disrupted by earthquakes.

b People living in tall buildings felt the tremors.

____

c Scientists use seismographs to measure vibrations.

____

d Smaller aftershocks sometimes follow the main quake.

____

e Two earthquakes on the seabed triggered waves up to 10 metres high.

____

f Seismologists use the Richter Scale to measure earthquakes.

____

g Scientists have identified earthquake 'hot spots'.

____

Punctuation—Single inverted commas for technical words

We often use **single inverted commas** when we use a **technical word**, but only the first time we use it.

Example It occurs where there is a '<u>fault</u>' or break in the earth's crust. The blocks on either side of the <u>fault</u> move up and down against each other, or shift lengthways.

This tells our reader that the word has a special, technical meaning in this context.

We don't usually use inverted commas for the name of the phenomenon we are explaining (e.g. tsunami). It is usually clear that this is a technical term by its use in the title of the text.

Extra! Do you know why Kenny used inverted commas for 'quake'? He wanted to show that the 'quake' part of 'earthquake' means vibration. He used the inverted commas to show he was taking this part of the word out of the full word, for this special reason.

Put the technical words in inverted commas where needed in this paragraph from a text explaining glaciers. Remember to use inverted commas the first time (only) you meet the technical word.

At the back end of a glacier, high up in the mountains, is a large basin called the neve. The neve is where the snow builds up and gets packed in ice. The long middle part of the glacier is called the trunk. The ice from the neve slowly flows downhill and adds to the trunk of the glacier. Eventually, ice from the trunk arrives at the front end of the glacier—the terminal. This is where the glacier melts, and comes out as a stream or river. As the glacier moves downhill it moves over humps and around bends in the valley. This causes the glacier ice to crack and buckle. The cracks formed are called crevasses. When the glacier flows down a steep drop an icefall is formed. An icefall is like a waterfall but is made of glacier ice.

COMMAS

It can be difficult to know when to use commas in the kind of long sentences you often need when explaining things. Sometimes a comma will seem necessary, but at other times it will interrupt the flow of ideas. Sometimes it will not matter if you use a comma or not.

The best idea is to read your writing out loud and with expression. You will often hear if you need a comma or not to make your ideas clear.

Can you help?

Can you help put in commas and full stops where you think they are needed in this second paragraph about glaciers? Remember: reading it out loud will help you.

Glaciers are like huge rivers of ice that come sliding down from the mountains high up in the alps layers and layers of snow build up and get pressed together into ice as the ice gets heavier and heavier it starts to slide downhill this moving ice is called a 'glacier' sometimes glaciers gradually expand and move forwards down the valleys into the sea but at other times they gradually shrink and move backwards up into the mountains when the front end of a glacier moves forwards we say it is 'advancing' and when it moves backwards we say it is 'retreating'.

Puzzle time

Can you write these disaster words into the no-clue-crossword spaces so that they all fit?

Tornado	Typhoon	Cyclone	Avalanche	Flood
Hurricane	Volcano	Blizzard	Earthquake	Drought

Do you know what all the words mean? Look up any you are not sure of in your dictionary.

Your turn to write

Tips for phenomenal writers

When writing an explanation, be sure you understand what you are trying to explain. Ask people questions (your teacher, your parents, for example) to be sure what happens when, why and how. Then try to explain the process to someone else, to check if your explanation is clear, BEFORE you put it in writing.

1. Below is some information in note form about tornadoes and a simple diagram. Read through the notes and look at the diagram. If you are not sure about anything, ask someone to help you. Then write an explanation following these stages:
   - statement of phenomenon
   - explanation of how or why
   - extra information
   - concluding comment (if you want).

   Note: You don't have to include all this information, and you can add information and ideas of your own.

- Tornadoes—also known as 'twisters' in United States
- Funnel-shaped tubes of rapidly spinning air—like huge swirling ropes of air
- Few hundred metres across
- Only last a short time—sometimes one hour
- Move at 10–60 kilometres an hour
- Usually happen when thunderstorms around—energy in huge thunderclouds spirals downwards—just like what happens as water spirals down the plughole in the bath
- Under right conditions—warm, humid air starts to rise upwards—at same time, very strong winds blow in opposite directions around rising air
- Whirling effect starts—whirling pushes air from centre (like clothes being spun in a washing machine)
- Leaves a core of low pressure in centre—low pressure like a powerful vacuum—sucks up everything in path
- Very destructive—can suck the walls of a house outwards so it collapses
- 500 to 600 tornadoes each year in US
- Also common in Australia
- *Twister*—popular film

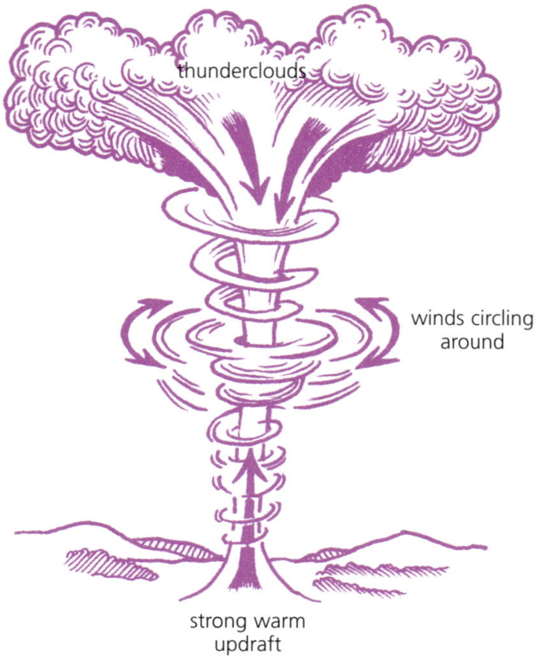

2 For extra practice, choose one of the natural phenomena from the box below and write a short explanation. Use your own paper or your Writer's Notebook.

- Do some research to find out about the phenomenon. Talk to someone if you need help to understand.
- Write a plan that includes the important things you need to mention.
- Draft your explanation following the stages in activity 1 above. Keep it simple—don't include every single detail.
- Read through your explanation as you go to make sure it is clear and makes sense.
- Give it to someone else to read when you finish your draft. Make changes if they did not understand something or if you left out important information.
- Proofread for spelling, punctuation and grammar.
- Write your explanation out properly and draw a picture to go with it.

What causes hail?
How does snow form?
What causes bushfires?
What causes rainbows?
What causes the greenhouse effect?
Why do avalanches happen?

Chapter 10 Writing a discussion

In a discussion, your aim is to present both sides of an issue (question) in a balanced way and then come to a conclusion.

STRUCTURE

LANGUAGE

Do superheroes make good role models for children?

1. Superman, the first comic book superhero, started leaping over tall buildings and stopping bullets with his chest in a 1938 comic book. Since then other superheroes have followed—the Phantom, Batman, Spiderman, Wonderwoman and the X-men, for example. These superheroes are certainly loved by most children, but are they good role models for their everyday lives?

2. Starting with the positives, superheroes always fight on the side of good. They spend their whole lives fighting to save and protect the world and its inhabitants. They never stray from the right path. Children can never be so perfect, but it is good for them to aim for such high moral standards.

3. Another positive is that superheroes never, ever, give up. They always fight on for good, no matter how hopeless things look. Even when the world is about to blow up, the superhero will go in just one last time to find the bomb and save the world from death and destruction. This teaches children to keep on trying when things are difficult.

4. Superheroes have many other good qualities that are good for children to see in action. Peter Parker (Spiderman), for example, is very kind to his old Aunt May. The X-men fight against the hate and prejudice of humans against mutants.

5. There are, however, some negative points to consider. For one thing, superheroes always win. Everything always turns out well in the end. This might give children false hope if they are in a bad situation. In the real world, things don't always work out the right way.

6. Another thing is that superheroes usually only win because they are extremely strong and have special powers. This could make children think that physical power can solve everything.

7. Superheroes may also make us overlook real life heroes—the fireman who saves a child's life, or just the many people who work hard every day for others. Ordinary heroes are not particularly strong or brave, they don't have special powers and they don't always win.

8. And finally, superheroes usually look ridiculous. They wear figure-hugging body-suits, very peculiar masks and gym shoes. They are certainly not good fashion role models!

9. I believe that, on balance, the benefits of superheroes as role models outweigh the drawbacks. Superheroes have good personal qualities and values, and that makes them excellent role models for children.

Statement of the issue

Arguments on one side—usually organised into paragraphs

Arguments on the other side

Each paragraph begins with a topic sentence and is developed with facts, opinions or examples

Conclusion sums up arguments and comes to a conclusion

Connectives

Words like *one, another, this, these* to ***connect ideas***

Present tense for giving views

Modals (e.g. *could, may*) and adverbs (e.g. *usually, certainly*) to show strength of opinion

Opinion adjectives

Mostly ***complex sentences***

What did you read?

1. Circle the best answer. What are *all* the positive arguments about?
   - **a** The qualities of superheroes
   - **b** The qualities of the stories they appear in
   - **c** How superheroes fight to save the world

2. According to the writer:
   - **a** Why is it good for children to see superheroes always keeping to the right path?

     ____

   - **b** How might superheroes help children to keep on trying in the face of difficulties?

     ____

   - **c** What is one difference about the way things happen in the world of superheroes and the real world? ____

3. Circle the best answer. Which argument for the negative is not serious?

   a first **b** second **c** third **d** fourth

4. Does the writer conclude for or against the question? ____________

   Do you agree or disagree? Give at least one reason. ____

   ____

How was it written?

1. You must state the issue at the start of the discussion, but it is good to give some background to the issue first. This writer tells us H ___ ___ L ___ ___ ___ comic book superheroes have been around, and the N ___ ___ ___ ___ of some well-known ones.

2. The writer gives the same amount of space to arguments for and arguments against. Why do you think this is a good idea? ____

3. Circle the best answer. There are a few ways to sum up arguments in the conclusion. This writer:
   - **a** summarises the arguments on the side she agrees with.
   - **b** mentions the main argument for and the main argument against.
   - **c** summarises all the arguments on both sides.

4. Words like ***one***, ***another***, ***other***, ***one other***, ***one more***, ***also*** and ***too*** help to link the arguments across the discussion. (They are a bit like the threads that sew up different pieces of material.) Underline these 'thread' words at the start of paragraphs 3, 4, 6 and 7.

5. Tick the things that helped you to follow the whole discussion.

   Arguments for separate from arguments against ____

   Separate paragraphs for each argument ____

   Topic sentences ____

   'Thread' words ____

   Conclusion ____

Spelling and meaning

superheroes	whole	perfect	moral	standards
positive	qualities	negative	prejudice	mutants
particularly	ridiculous	benefits	drawbacks	balance

Tip for simply superheroic spellers
Don't rely ONLY on a computer spell-check to get the spelling right when you type. If you write the sentence *They spend their hole lives saving the world*, the spell-check will not pick up that you wrongly used ***hole*** (meaning "space") instead of ***whole*** (meaning "complete"). The spell-check only looks at the word, not the meaning of the word in the sentence.

1 Choose words from the word box to match the clues.

a Opposite of ***part*** ______________________
b Synonym for ***advantages*** ______________________
c Synonym for ***silly*** ______________________
d Synonym for ***disadvantages*** ______________________
e Adjective describing something with no faults ______________________
f Positive features or characteristics ______________________
g To do with good and bad behaviour ______________________
h Creatures produced by a genetic change ______________________
i An adverb meaning the same as ***especially*** ______________________
j Rules of behaviour ______________________
k An unfair opinion formed without thought or knowledge ______________________
l Something used to weigh things ______________________

2 Most words ending in a consonant +***o*** add ***es*** to form the plural (e.g. ***superhero → superheroes***). Exceptions are ***pianos***, ***photos***, ***solos***. Can you unscramble these ***-oes*** words?

a MOTTAOES ______________________
b TOPTAOES ______________________
c CANLOVOES ______________________
d CEHOES ______________________
e OSQMUITOES ______________________
f ROTPEDOES ______________________
g GMANOES ______________________
h REHOES ______________________

3 There are many words to talk about the arguments **for** and the arguments **against** in a discussion. Can you add the missing words to this table?

For	Against
Advantages	
Pluses	
	Negatives
Benefits	D
Affirmative case (used in debating)	N case

Grammar—Modals and adverbs

When we write discussions or expositions, we often need to show how strongly we believe something or how sure we are about what we say.

One way we do this is by using **modals** such as ***can, might, may, could, will, should*** and ***must*** in the verb group.

Examples This might give children false hope if they are in a bad situation.
Superheroes may also make us overlook real life heroes.

Another way is by using **adverbs** such as ***definitely, really, perhaps, maybe, surely, certainly, possibly, probably, likely, always, never, usually, often*** and ***sometimes***.

Examples These superheroes are certainly loved by most children ...
... superheroes usually look ridiculous

Often we use **modals and adverbs together** to show what we think.

Example Children can never be so perfect ...

We can also show how strongly we feel by NOT using a modal.

Example This teaches children to keep on trying is stronger and more definite than This may teach children to keep on trying.

Look at the sentences below. For each group, write:

- 1 for the strongest, most certain opinion
- 3 for the weakest, least certain opinion
- 2 for the opinion in between.

a The Phantom is definitely the best superhero ever. ____
The Phantom is probably the best superhero ever. ____
The Phantom may be the best superhero ever. ____

b We should encourage children to watch films like *Spiderman*. ____
We must encourage children to watch films like *Spiderman*. ____
We could encourage children to watch films like *Spiderman*. ____

c Children could copy the behaviour of superheroes. ____
Children are sure to copy the behaviour of superheroes. ____
Children might possibly copy the behaviour of superheroes. ____

d Parents should always stop children watching these shows. ____
Parents should perhaps stop children watching these shows. ____
Parents should probably stop children watching these shows. ____

JOKE

Q. What's the difference between a normal man and Superman?

A. A normal man wears his undies underneath his pants!

Punctuation—Apostrophe of possession

We use an **apostrophe** to show that a person or thing **owns or possesses** another.

Example a child's life = the life of a child

People often get confused about when and where to use the apostrophe of possession, but it is really very simple.

When to use it

You ONLY use the apostrophe when one person or thing owns another.

Examples Superman saves his friend's house. ✓ (The friend owns the house, so you need an apostrophe.)
Superman has two good friend's. ✗ (The friends own nothing in this sentence, so you don't need an apostrophe—*friends* is simply plural.)
Superman has two good friends. ✓

Where to put it

You only have to remember ONE thing about where to put the apostrophe of possession.

Put the apostrophe immediately after the person or thing that does the possessing.

Examples A friend's house = the house of a <u>friend</u> → apostrophe goes after *friend* → friend's

My parents' house = the house of my <u>parents</u> → apostrophe goes after *parents* → parents'

The children's house = the house of the <u>children</u> → apostrophe goes after *children* → children's

That's it! No need to think about singulars and plurals. Just ask yourself: Who or what does the owning? *Then* put the apostrophe.

Put the apostrophes where needed in these sentences. (Some sentences don't need any.)

a Phantoms horse is called Hero.
b Supermans best friends were Lois Lane and Jimmy Olsen.
c It was the three villains last attempt to get rid of Batman.
d Many childrens television shows have no real heroes.
e Adults usually admire the superheroes devotion to duty.
f The X-mens fight against evil never seems to end.
g The films ending is a surprise.
h Fans can get more information about their superhero on the website.
i Batmans cave is beneath the city of Gotham City.
j Many different actors have played Superman.

Can you help?

This student's paragraph is missing all its punctuation. Can you put the punctuation back where it is needed? *Hint:* There are quotation marks (to show the words someone says) missing in one sentence.

Superheroes can be our guides in everyday life most peoples lives even childrens lives involve tough decisions when faced with these decisions we can ask ourselves what would superman do I dont mean what special superpowers he would use but what choices he would make in the same situation superheroes have to make some very difficult decisions in do-or-die life-or-death situations of course their decisions might be more critical than the ones we have to make but they can still teach us something about the responsible way to act

Puzzle time

1 How many superhero words can you find in this wordsearch. The words might be the names of superheroes, their real identities, the villains they fight or something to do with their special powers.

S	P	B	Z	R	P	H	A	N	T	O	M	P	M
U	R	O	B	I	N	J	V	U	L	T	U	R	E
P	A	F	A	K	R	Y	P	T	O	N	I	T	E
E	B	A	T	G	I	R	L	B	X	E	N	A	O
R	P	X	M	H	D	S	L	O	M	M	U	K	J
W	G	E	A	H	I	O	L	K	E	B	V	F	D
O	E	R	N	G	U	I	K	F	N	H	G	T	S
M	Q	W	P	G	O	T	H	A	M	C	I	T	Y
A	X	Z	B	S	U	P	E	R	M	A	N	L	K
N	G	H	J	S	P	I	D	E	R	M	A	N	H
W	O	L	V	E	R	I	N	E	W	V	B	A	M

2 How many words can you make from SPIDERMAN? Write them on your own paper.

Your turn to write

Tips for supersonic, superpowered writers

Prepare for writing a discussion by brainstorming points for and against, without worrying too much about how strong or weak they are. Then look through them and choose two or three strong points to use in your discussion.

1 Here are three entertainment topics. For each topic, brainstorm at least two arguments for and two arguments against, using the table below.

Video and computer games are good for children.
Reading a book is better than seeing a film.
Bart Simpson is a good role model for children.

Topic	Fors	Againsts
Video and computer games are good for children.		
Reading a book is better than seeing a film.		
Bart Simpson is a good role model for children.		

2 Now choose one topic and draft a discussion about it in the space below.

- State the issue clearly at the beginning.
- Organise your arguments into **fors** and **againsts**.
- Write a topic sentence for each argument.
- Develop the arguments with examples and other details.
- Use connectives and 'thread' words to link your arguments.
- Use modals and adverbs to show how strongly you feel.
- Say which side you agree with in your conclusion.

Revise your draft, checking grammar, spelling and punctuation, and then write it out again in your Writer's Notebook.

The issue

Arguments for

Arguments against

Your conclusion

Answers on pages 99–100

Chapter 11 Writing for school research projects

This chapter aims to help you with school projects. It is organised differently from the other chapters in the book. It has three sections:

- Using your own words
- Writing imaginative texts based on facts
- Referencing

You will see how one student worked on a Year 6 project on the topic of "Chinese Festivals and Customs", and you will do some work on this topic too.

Your turn to write

Tips for perfectly polished project writers

- Don't be tempted to just cut and paste from a web page to make your own text. You won't end up with a good piece of writing, and your teacher will be able to see it is not your own work.
- Instead, select information and put it into your own words to show you understand what you are writing about.
- Think about writing an imaginative text based on factual information—for example, a diary or a narrative—as well as factual reports and recounts.
- Make sure you say exactly where you got your information. Write down the details of a book or website as soon as you use it. This will save you having to find it again at the end of your project.

Using your own words

Here is some information about Chinese New Year that our student found on a website. Look at the next page to see how he selected from the information and changed the words to make his own text. You don't have to read this text in detail—look mainly at the parts marked with lines to the next page.

Chinese New Year

Chinese New Year starts with the New Moon on the first day of the new year and ends on the full moon 15 days later. The 15th day of the new year is called the Lantern Festival, which is celebrated at night with lantern displays and children carrying lanterns in a parade.

The Chinese calendar is based on a combination of lunar and solar movements. The lunar cycle is about 29.5 days. In order to 'catch up' with the solar calendar the Chinese insert an extra month every few years (seven years out of a 19-year cycle). This is the same as adding an extra day on a leap year. This is why, according to the solar calendar, the Chinese New Year falls on a different date each year.

New Year's Eve and New Year's Day are celebrated as a family affair, a time of reunion and thanksgiving. Ancestors are greatly respected in Chinese culture because they are responsible for laying the foundations for the fortune and glory of the family. Their presence is acknowledged on New Year's Eve with a dinner arranged for them at the family banquet table. The spirits of the ancestors, together with the living, celebrate the onset of the New Year as one great community. The communal feast is called 'surrounding the stove' or 'weilu'. It symbolises family unity and honours the past and present generations.

The 15-day celebration

Every day of the Lunar New Year has a special significance. The first day, for example, is the 'welcoming of the gods of the heavens and earth'. Many people abstain from meat on the first day of the new year because it is believed that this will ensure long and happy lives for them.

On the second day, the Chinese pray to their ancestors as well as to all the gods. They are extra kind to dogs and feed them well, as it is believed that the second day is the birthday of all dogs.

The fifth day is called 'po woo'. On that day people stay home to welcome the God of Wealth. No one visits families and friends on the fifth day because it will bring both parties bad luck. On the sixth to the 10th day, the Chinese visit their relatives and friends freely. They also visit the temples to pray for good fortune and health.

The seventh day is considered the birthday of human beings. Noodles are eaten to promote longevity and raw fish for success.

The 10th day to the 12th are days that friends and relatives should be invited for dinner. After so much rich food, on the 13th day you should have simple rice congee and mustard greens (choi sum) to cleanse the system.

The 14th day should be for preparations to celebrate the Lantern festival, which is to be held on the 15th night.

Adapted from web page *Chinese New Year*, www.educ.uvic.ca/faculty/mroth/438/CHINA/Chinese_new_year

WHAT THE STUDENT DID

- Wrote a sentence to introduce the topic
- Made up own sentences where needed
- Changed order of information
- Left out information he did not understand
- Left out some small details
- Used own words as much as possible
- Gave the name of the website—full details will be in his bibliography
- Selected from examples given—did not use all
- Changed order of words
- Added his own comment to round off the report

STUDENT'S TEXT

CHINESE NEW YEAR

Chinese New Year is a very important time for Chinese people. It starts on the first New Moon of the year and begins a 15 day period of celebration until the Full Moon. The New Year falls on a different date each year, because it is based on the Chinese calendar. This calendar is based on the movements of the sun and the moon.

Chinese people celebrate New Year's Eve and New Year's Day as a family affair. It is a time of reunion and thanksgiving. Ancestors, who are greatly respected in Chinese culture, are remembered on New Year's Eve with a dinner at the family banquet table. The spirits of the ancestors celebrate the New Year together with the living as one whole community. The communal feast is called 'surrounding the stove', or 'weilu' in Chinese, and is a symbol of family unity. (*Chinese New Year*, website)

Every day for 15 days after New Year's Day, there are rituals and celebrations of different kinds. For example, on the first day, people welcome the gods of heaven and earth. They do not eat meat because they believe it will give them long and happy life. The fifth day is called 'po woo', and people stay home to welcome the God of Wealth. Nobody visits anyone else because it will bring bad luck. The seventh day is considered to be the birthday of all humans. (*Chinese New Year*, website)

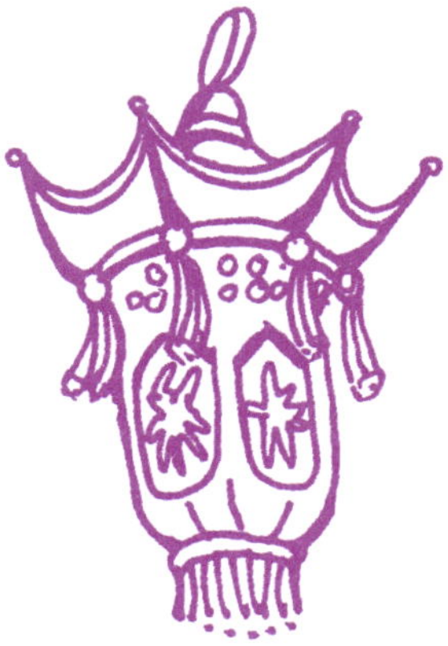

On the last day, the Lantern Festival is held at night. There are lantern displays everywhere and children carry lanterns in a parade.

Chinese New Year sounds like great fun and much more interesting than the Western way of celebrating.

1 Read these three paragraphs about Chinese New Year from another website.* Complete the sentences about each using your own words. You may need to leave out some of the information.

a Of all the traditional Chinese festivals, the New Year was perhaps the most elaborate, colourful and important. This was a time for the Chinese to congratulate each other and themselves on having passed through another year, a time to finish out the old, and to welcome in the new year.

Chinese New Year is ______________________________ of all Chinese festivals.

Chinese people ______________________________

______________________________ and welcome

____

b Preparations for the traditional Chinese New Year in old China started well before New Year's Day. The 20th of the Twelfth Moon (or month) was set aside for the annual housecleaning or the 'sweeping of the grounds'. After the house was cleaned, it was time to bid farewell to the Kitchen God or Zaowang—the guardian of the family hearth. By tradition, the Kitchen God left the house on the 23rd of the last month to report on the behaviour of the family. At this time, the family did everything possible to obtain a good report from the Kitchen God. On the evening of the 23rd, they would give the Kitchen God a farewell dinner with sweet foods and honey.

In the traditional Chinese New Year, preparations started well beforehand. One day was set aside for

______________________________.

After this, the family ______________________________.

Everyone was very well behaved at this time because ______________________________

______________________________.

On the 23rd they farewelled ______________________________

____

c In the Lantern Festival, people carried lanterns into the streets to take part in a great parade. Young men would highlight the parade with a dragon dance. The dragon was made of bamboo, silk and paper and might stretch for more than 30 metres in length. The bobbing and the weaving of the dragon was an impressive sight, and formed a fitting finish to the New Year festival.

One of the ______________________________ parts of the New Year was the

______________________________. Everyone carried

______________________________ and took part in

______________________________. The highlight of the parade was

______________________________. The dragon

____

*Texts on this page are adapted from *Celebration of the Chinese New Year*, Chinese Culture Foundation, www.c-c-c.org/chineseculture/festival/newyear/newyear.html

2. Read this interesting text about the Chinese animal zodiac. Then complete the shorter version below using the information and some of your own words.

The Chinese animal zodiac

The Chinese animal zodiac is a 12-year cycle used for dating the years. It represents a cyclical concept of time (based on the cycles of the moon), rather than the Western linear concept of time. Every year is assigned an animal name or 'sign' according to a repeating cycle: Rat, Ox, Tiger, Rabbit, Dragon, Snake, Horse, Sheep (or Ram), Monkey, Rooster, Dog and Pig (or Boar).

Horoscopes have developed around the animal signs, much like monthly horoscopes in the West have been developed for the different moon signs, Pisces, Aries, etc. For example, a Chinese horoscope may predict that a person born in the Year of the Horse would be "cheerful, popular, and loves to compliment others".

According to Chinese legend, the twelve animals quarrelled one day as to who was to head the cycle of years. The gods were asked to decide and they held a contest: whoever was to reach the opposite bank of the river would be first, and the rest of the animals would receive their years according to their finish. All the twelve animals gathered at the river bank and jumped in. Unknown to the ox, the rat had jumped upon his back. As the ox was about to jump ashore, the rat jumped off the ox's back, and won the race. The pig, who was very lazy, ended up last. That is why the rat is the first year of the animal cycle, the ox second and the pig last.

Which animal sign rules your birth year? What about other people you know?

Rat	1948	1960	1972	1984	1996	2008
Ox	1949	1961	1973	1985	1997	2009
Tiger	1950	1962	1974	1986	1998	2010
Rabbit	1951	1963	1975	1987	1999	2011
Dragon	1952	1964	1976	1988	2000	2012
Snake	1953	1965	1977	1989	2001	2013
Horse	1954	1966	1978	1990	2002	2014
Sheep	1955	1967	1979	1991	2003	2015
Monkey	1956	1968	1980	1992	2004	2016
Rooster	1957	1969	1981	1993	2005	2017
Dog	1958	1970	1982	1994	2006	2018
Boar	1959	1971	1983	1995	2007	2019

In the Chinese calendar, every year in a ______________________________ is given an ____________________, for example ______________________________ ____________________. ____________________ have developed for these animal signs, much like ______________________________ for the different moon signs. For example, ____________________ born in the Year of the Horse ______________________________ ______________________________. There is ______________________________ that explains the order of the animal signs. The gods ______________________________ to work out who should head the cycle of years. The rat used his cunning by ____________________ and won ____________________. The pig came last because ____________________.
That is why ______________________________.
My animal sign is ____________________. What is ____________________?

RESEARCH IDEA
You might like to do some more research to find out what the animal means about your character and personality. If you are searching the Internet, you could type in "Chinese animal signs" or "year of the ...." (for whatever animal sign you are).

Writing imaginative texts based on facts

It can be interesting to write imaginative kinds of texts based on factual information in school projects. For example, for this project, you could write a diary of someone's experiences over the New Year festival period.

Use the information from the texts so far and from the new text below to write an imaginative diary in the space on the next page. Use the ideas given if you want, but add ideas from your own imagination as well.

Traditional taboos and superstitions of Chinese New Year

House cleaning

The entire house should be cleaned before New Year's Day. On New Year's Eve, all brooms, brushes and other cleaning equipment are put away. Sweeping or dusting should not be done on New Year's Day for fear that good fortune will be swept away. After New Year's Day, the floors may be swept. There are many superstitions about the way to sweep. For example, if you sweep the dirt out over the threshold, you will sweep one of the family away. Also, to sweep the dust and dirt out of your house by the front entrance is to sweep away the good fortune of the family. All dirt and rubbish must be taken out the back door.

Bringing in the New Year and expelling the Old

Shooting off firecrackers on New Year's Eve is the Chinese way of sending out the Old Year and welcoming in the New Year. On the stroke of midnight on New Year's Eve, every door in the house, and even windows, have to be open to allow the old year to go out.

Personal appearances and cleanliness

On New Year's Day, we are not supposed to wash our hair because it would mean we would have washed away good luck for the New Year. Red clothing is preferred during this festive occasion. Red is considered a bright, happy colour, sure to bring the wearer a sunny and bright future. It is believed that appearance and attitude during New Year's Day sets the tone for the rest of the year. Children and unmarried friends, as well as close relatives, are given 'lai see', little red envelopes with crisp one dollar bills inserted, for good fortune.

Adapted from *Taboos and Superstitions of Chinese New Year*, www.educ.uvic.ca/faculty/mroth/438/CHINA/taboos.html

My diary

• Sweeping of the grounds • In trouble for sweeping wrong way	Friday
• Farewell to Kitchen God • Everyone kind to each other • Farewell dinner—yummy food	Sunday
• New Year's Eve • Special dinner • Honour ancestors • Fire crackers	Tuesday
• New Year's Day • The Year of the ____ • Red clothes • 'Lai see' envelopes	Wednesday
• 7th day of New Year—everyone's birthday • Everyone eats too much	Wednesday
• Lantern Festival • Parade • Dragon dance • End of festival	Thursday

Referencing

It is very important to say where you got your information from (e.g. which book, which website, which newspaper article). This is called **referencing**.

You need to give a reference:

- when you quote **someone's exact words** AND when you put **someone else's information** into your own words
- **on the page** you use the information AND **in the bibliography** at the end.

The student who wrote about the Chinese New Year twice gave the name of the web page he got his information from: *Chinese New Year*, web page.

- If he had known the name of the web page author, he would have written that instead of the title of the web page.
- If he had used information from a book he would have given just the author's surname and date (e.g. Brown, 2003).

In his bibliography, he gave the full details of the web page:

Chinese New Year, (web page) www.educ.uvic.ca/faculty/mroth/438/CHINA/Chinese_new_year.html)

Here is his full bibliography.

Type	Bibliography	Notes
Website	• Chinese New Year, (website) www.educ.uvic.ca/faculty/mroth/438/CHINA/Chinese_new_year.html (no date)	List in alphabetical order by author's name
Website	• Chinese Culture Foundation, *Celebration of the Chinese New Year* (website) www.c-c-c.org/chineseculture/festival/newyear/newyear.html (no date)	Put organisation if no person given as author
Book	• Grahame, M., 1995, *The Chinese Zodiac*. Brown Publishing Company, Sydney	Give the date of publication; if you can't find one, write "no date".
Book	• Jones, J. and King, L., 2001, *Festivals of the World*. Hector Publishing, Melbourne	Put titles in *italics* if typing ("quotation marks" if handwriting)
Newspaper article	• Larsen, R. "It's the Year of the Monkey", *The Gazette* 3/1/04	

Can you write these materials as a bibliography? Remember to put them in alphabetical order.

A book called Festivals, by Jenny Bilson, published in 1999 in London by Slater Publishing
A website called Chinese Calendar, by Scotland Online, www.new-year.co.uk/chinese/calendar
A newspaper article headed Which year were you born? by Kyle Tyson, which appeared in the Northern News on the 10th January 2004

Your turn to write

You might be doing a research project at school right now. If so, keep this chapter close by to help you. If you are not working on a project, choose any topic you like to research and write up. Perhaps you could research and write about the culture and customs of a country you are interested in.

Answers

Chapter 1 — Pages 2–9

What did you read?

1 **a** two; **b** Roald Amundsen; **c** He saw the Norwegian flag flying.
2 Bad—they were not suited for the long journey or the deep snow.
3 exhausted, disappointed
4 the rations slowly ran out
5 His diary suggests he knew they were going to die: "I do not think we can hope for any better things now."

How was it written?

1 You should have ticked: Who it is about; What job or position the person had; What the person had done before; What the person wanted to do; The period in which the events happened; Where the events took place
2 **a** In the early 20th century; **b** In 1910; **c** from this point on; **d** Three weeks later
4 You might have said something like: The diary was interesting and moving—it clearly showed the terrible way the men died. It also showed that Scott really was a hero, just as William says in his conclusion.

Spelling and meaning

2 **a** exploration; **b** expedition; **c** ambition; **d** devotion
3 **a** courage; **b** hardship; **c** perish; **d** blizzard; **e** rations; **f** obstacles
4 **a** courageous; **b** heroic; **c** adventurous; **d** determined; **e** extraordinary; **f** bold; **g** experienced; **h** brilliant; **i** gallant; **j** daring

Grammar

Amelia Earhart was born in Kansas in the [United States of America] in 1898. She was just five years old when Orville and Wilbur Wright made their famous flight at Kitty Hawk in North Carolina. Little did she know then that she would be just as famous in the history of aviation as the [Wright Brothers.]
In 1932, [Earhart] flew out of New Brunswick on the east coast of Canada aiming for Paris. She wanted to be the first person to successfully make a flight across the Atlantic Ocean. Unfortunately, a severe storm forced her to land in Ireland, rather than [Paris], but she had still achieved her goal. Sadly, she was dead only five years later, as she attempted to be the first person to circumnavigate the world. She struck trouble over the Pacific Ocean, just east of the International Dateline, and disappeared.
Thirty years later, the search for her plane was renewed. On a small island just south of the [Equator], a navigator's bookcase and part of a woman's shoe were found. It seems likely they belonged to this very brave aviation pioneer.

Punctuation

1 **a** As a young boy, Ernest Shackleton longed for adventure and excitement.
b Despite all the hardships, they were determined to continue their voyage.
c After a slow journey through pack ice, their ship finally reached its destination.
d In 1778, Captain James Cook was the most famous explorer of his time.
e In 1871, David Livingstone, the greatest African explorer of all time, had been missing for six years.
f The *New York Herald* sent Henry Stanley, an experienced reporter, to find Livingstone.
2 **a** There were four dogs: Henry, Jacky, Nino and Nina.
b He wrote: "I can't go on any further."
c The trip has three stages: sailing there, climbing the mountains and setting up camp.
d Remember these things: travel in a group, let someone know your route and take a safety kit.
e His first words were: "Welcome to you all."

Can you help?

a/1, b/5, b/2, d/3, e/6, f/7, g/4

Puzzle time

Chapter 2 — Pages 10–17

What did you read?

1. Because three relatives had died in Aunt Bessie's care
2. A sign of danger approaching
3. c
4. To ask her to ring and keep her aunt on the phone so that she could get rid of the meal
5. Being read a bedtime story that is for much younger children
6. c
7. our relatives

How was it written?

1. I would tick all three.
2. Aunt Bessie hugging her (suffocating her), feeding her (poisoning her), reading to her (torturing her)
3. **a** thundering; **b** sliced; **c** rattled; **d** grasped; **e** mounted; **f** slipped;
4. **a** The idea of a terrifying death sliced through my heart like a cold, sharp blade.
   b A definite sign!
   c What would Charlie's Angels do in a situation like this?
   d Horror of horrors!

Spelling and meaning

1. **a** squirmed; **b** situation, responsible; **c** alert; **d** announced; **e** oblivious; **f** obviously, accident; **g** crippling; **h** stomach
2. **a** legs; **b** heart; **c** knees; **d** blood; **e** throats; **f** face; **g** ears

Grammar

1. **a** Bianca babysits her little sister, Yoli, every afternoon.
   b My Uncle Ernie always rings up during our favourite telly program.
   c You can watch the nature documentary.
   d He talks for a very long time.
   e Sometimes she is very naughty.
   f Sasha and Julia stay with their cousins in the country every Christmas.
   g You can go to bed right now.
   h Their cousins never come to visit them in the city.
2. b/d: My Uncle Ernie always rings up during our favourite telly program, and (he) talks for a very long time.
   c/f: You can watch the nature documentary or you can go to bed right now.
   e/f: Sasha and Julia stay with their cousins in the country every Christmas, but their cousins never come to visit them in the city.
3. **a** My Aunty Dora makes soup that smells like rotten fish.
   b I can hardly breathe when my Uncle Vinnie gives me his famous bear hugs.
   c I love my great grandmother because she tells funny stories.
   d My cousins and I end up fighting every time we get together.
   e Mum always gives us a lecture about being polite before we visit our Aunty Zita.

Puzzle time

The Artful Dodger: *Oliver Twist*
Christopher Robin: *Winnie the Pooh*
Erica Yurken: *Hating Alison Ashley*
Peter, Susan, Edmund and Lucy: *The Lion, the Witch and the Wardrobe*

Dorothy: *The Wizard of Oz*
The Oompa Loompas: *Charlie and the Chocolate Factory*
The Lost Boys: *Peter Pan and Wendy*
Captain Haddock: *Tintin*
Bunyip Bluegum: *The Magic Pudding*
The Mad Hatter: *Alice's Adventures in Wonderland*
Mole, Rat, Badger and Toad: *Wind in the Willows*
Miss Trunchbull: *Matilda*

Chapter 3 Pages 18–25

What did you read?

1 b
2 drifting
3 When you cook, you make things hotter. When you put on blankets, you get hotter. So maybe the heat from the blankets would 'cook' dreams.
4 a and d
5 the sound of wind as the rider rides
6 (Possible answers) "I lie straight": content, happy, peaceful; "Drifting off": sleepy, happy, calm; "My bike": excited, happy, free

How were they written?

1 **a** brushes, floats down, settles; **b** swooping, flying
2 **a** a whisper; **b** a fox; **c** a boat
3 **a** i dusk; ii smooth path; iii tyres hum; iv no hands; v tailwind; **b** speed

Spelling and meaning

1 **a** through; **b** threw; **c** tire; **d** tyre; **e** straight; **f** strait; **g** court; **h** caught
2 **c** breeze, straight, search, possums, through, swooping, tyres, bruises, quiet, caught, curled, smooth
3 Possible answers: **a** whack—a newspaper hitting something, a smack; **b** wham—a boxer falling to the floor; **c** wheeze—a person breathing hard; **d** whimper—a child crying, a dog crying; **e** whine—a person complaining; **f** whinge—a person complaining; **g** whip—the wind; **h** whirr—helicopter blades; **i** whiz—a fast ride at a fun park; **j** whoop—children playing a game, a bird's cry

Grammar

2 **a** The wind is a whip.
b Sleep is a soft cocoon.
c Dancing is freedom.
d Chocolate cake is heaven.
e Exams are torture.

Punctuation

1 There is not one right answer because it is your response to the poem. However, you might have said:
a smooth, flowing
b The punctuation makes you read it in a way that reflects the sheet falling.
c Because the feeling does not end/to keep the peaceful, dreamy feeling
2 Again there is not one right answer, but you might have said:
a quickly
b The punctuation makes you read it in a way that reflects the bike riding.
c It emphasises the excitement.

Can you help?

3 There is no one right answer, but here is one way to punctuate "Summer at the pool".

Splash!
Down down,
straighten out now,
What a dive!
Sweet, sweet, coolness
up now up,
floating like driftwood
thick silent peace
mmmm.
Splash!
Peace over,
time for fun!

Puzzle time

a An old woman swallowed a fly.
b Jack built a house.
c Isabel met an enormous bear, but didn't care.
d My mother said you should never play with the gypsies in the wood.
e The Owl and the Pussycat went to sea in a beautiful pea-green boat.
f Wynken, Blynken and Nod sailed off in a

wooden shoe one night.

g The Jumblies went to sea in a sieve.

h The Pobble has no toes, but once had as many as we.

i Matilda told such dreadful lies, it made one gasp and stretch one's eyes.

j Belinda lived in a little white house with a little black kitten …

Chapter 4 Pages 26–33

What did you read?

1 b

2 Level 1: services like sewerage, water, electricity, air conditioning and gas; Level 2: factories and storage; Level 3: living area

3 **a** sides of a cardboard box; **b** polystyrene; **c** dark blue tissue paper; **d** thin rubber tubing; **e** bubble wrap; **f** Easter egg packaging; **g** plastic sheeting; **h** clear plastic biscuit packaging

4 **a** False; **b** True; **c** False

How was it written?

1 **a** first paragraph; **b** second paragraph

2 order; We started; The first level; Then we worked on the second level; Next, we made the third level; Finally

3 **a** The students did not think tall skyscrapers would be suitable out at sea.

b They did not think cars would be used in a sea-city.

4 positive

Spelling and meaning

1 **a** basic, basis, basement;
b electric, electrical, electrify;
c unreal, unrealistic, reality

2 **a** lightweight; **b** approximately; **c** silos; **d** skyscrapers; **e** basically; **f** height; **g** design; **h** materials; **i** electricity; **j** realistic; **k** vehicles; **l** decided; **m** measuring; **n** cylinders

3 **a** whether; **b** weather; **c** allowed; **d** aloud; **e** which; **f** witch; **g** quiet; **h** piece; **i** peace; **j** board; **k** bored

Grammar

1 In Term 2 Class 6M were asked to construct a bridge out of paper that could hold up as much weight as possible. The bridge had to span a distance of 10 centimetres. Chris Learned's was the best. Chris managed to hold up 1 kilogram without his paper collapsing. Other students who tried to hold up 1 kilogram failed because of their design. Chris made his bridge with a section shaped like an unused staple. Our bridge held up 375 grams which was the second largest mass.

2 **a** glue, tape, fix; **b** build, construct; **c** begin, commence; **d** rotate, twist, invert; **e** place, stand; **f** view, observe

Punctuation

a odd-shaped; **b** ice-cold, red-hot; **c** multi-storey; **d** re-use; **e** eight-sided; **f** multi-purpose

Can you help?

a/2, b/5, c/1, d/6, e/3, f/7, g/8, h/4

Here is the full text:

Our task was to build a tower using only ten sheets of newspaper and sticky tape. The tower had to be rigid and stand up by itself. The tallest free standing tower would be the winner. Our idea was to tightly roll the paper into tubes. We did this process four times and then decided to strengthen the tower by doubling the newspaper. We also used tape to stick the tower to the table. When Mr Guilfoyle measured the towers, ours was three metres high and was the winning tower. It was very thin but very rigid.

Puzzle time

1 **a** cylindrical; **b** rectangular; **c** spherical; **d** oval; **e** conical; **f** pyramid-shaped; **g** cubic; **h** circular; **i** triangular; **j** octagonal; **k** hexagonal; **l** pentagonal

2 **a** Atlantis; **b** Neptune; **c** Poseidon

Chapter 5 Pages 34–41

What did you read?

1 Joe wants Ms Nori to help get a skateboarding ramp built in his area.

2 c
3 b
4 Five reasons including the last one.
5 No one correct answer, although you might think his last point would be the most persuasive for Ms Nori, who would be thinking of the whole community, not just young people.
6 Any of the following answers: It was designed by local skateboarders. / It is a place where big kids help little kids to learn to skate. / It is safe.

How was it written?

1 c
2 Perhaps because he thinks it is an especially good reason, and also because it sums up all his other arguments.
3 b
4 c
5 There is no one correct answer, but you might say yes, because the letter was clear, or because it was polite and friendly, or because Joe showed how strongly he felt and how much he loved skateboarding.

Spelling and meaning

1 **a** their; **b** They're; **c** There; **d** there; **e** They're, their, there
2 **a** ungrateful; **b** insignificant; **c** unselfish; **d** immobile; **e** imperfect; **f** impersonal; **g** impolite; **h** unimpressive; **i** inactive; **j** inadequate; **k** indirect; **l** ineffective
3 **a** snowboard, surfboard, ironing-board, boardroom, cardboard
b snowflake, snowboard, snowboarder, snowball, snowdrop, snowdrift, snowfall, snowfield
c surfboard, surfboat, surf-lifesaver, channel-surf, surf-ski
d windbreak, windbag, windburn, windblown, windchill, windcheater, windmill, windscreen, windshield, windswept, windjammer

Grammar

1 **a** sensible; **b** beautiful; **c** brilliant; **d** sad; **e** entertaining; **f** boring
2 **Good:** positive, brilliant, useful, excellent, clever; **Bad:** useless, unhelpful, shocking, negative, harmful; **Beautiful:** glorious, gorgeous, attractive, splendid, magnificent; **Ugly:** unattractive, revolting, unpleasant, terrible, disgusting

Punctuation

2 **a** I believe it's a really terrible plan.
b The group wants you to know its honest opinion.
c Most people who object to its construction don't know the facts.
d One thousand people say it's an excellent place for a skatepark.
e Its success will depend on its size, its design and its location.
f It's been talked about for long enough. It's time for action.

Can you help?

2. Nearly every netball game, someone slips over. There have been some serious injuries because people have slipped over.
5. Many people have complained about this before and I think it's time someone did something about it.
4. This should not keep happening. Someone should do something about it. They should rip up the old grass and lay down new grass. They could put a cover or something over the courts because the main reason there is no grass is because the rain washes it away.
3. In fact, you could even ask one of my friends who tripped over in a game and twisted her knee. She had to have an operation to put it back in place. She couldn't play for the rest of the season. It is very painful and she has to use crutches.
1. I am writing to complain that the Lapstone grass netball courts are in a terrible condition. There is sand and dirt everywhere.

Puzzle time

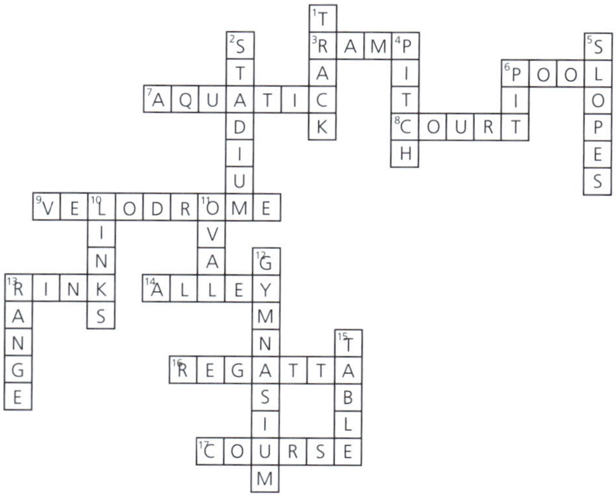

Your turn to write

Possible answers are:

1 **a** local newspaper, local Council member or mayor

b local newspaper; local Council member or mayor; local member of state/territory Parliament

c local or major newspaper; member of Parliament in charge of environment

d local newspaper; local member of state/territory Parliament; local member of federal Parliament

e major newspaper; local member of federal Parliament; prime minister

f major newspaper; member of Parliament in charge of education; state premier or territory chief minister

g local newspaper; member of Parliament in charge of education; state premier or territory chief minister

Chapter 6 Pages 42–49

What did you read?

1 **a** False; **b** False; **c** True; **d** False; **e** True

2 hydrogen bombs

3 how hot they are

4 light years

5 b

How was it written?

1 c

2 The words ***star*** and ***stars*** are used 22 times (23 if you count the title of the report).

3 **a** What are stars?; **b** Our Sun; **c** How they die

4 headings, paragraphs, topic sentences

5 Because they are personal comments and opinions and these are not relevant in an information report where the focus should be on facts.

6 These words are defined: light years, supernovae, black holes. You might have wanted the author to define any of the other words, but perhaps an explanation of the word 'nuclear' is the one that would most help readers. (It is probably not defined because it would be very difficult to define it in a few simple words.)

Spelling and meaning

1 **a** enormous; **b** powerful; **c** spectacular; **d** massive; **e** unimaginable; **f** temperature

2 **a** rotate; **b** million; **c** gravity; **d** difference; **e** collapse

3 **a** phenomenon—something interesting or unusual that has been observed

b phantom—ghostly apparition

c phase—stage in a process

d philosopher—someone who uses reason to understand humans and their world

e phoenix—imaginary bird in ancient stories

f phony—fake, unreal

g prophet—someone who predicts the future

h phrase—short group of words

i sphere—solid round object or shape

j trophy—prize or award

4 **a** botanist; **b** biologist; **c** geologist; **d** physicist; **e** chemist

Grammar

Corrections are underlined:

b Meteors are sometimes called 'shooting stars' but <u>they are</u> not really <u>stars</u>.

c Some meteors are coloured, mostly blue and white, though <u>they</u> might sometimes be red or green.

d A communication satellite bounces signals from one point on Earth to another point.

e Galaxies are vast clusters of thousands of millions of stars. They are classified according to their shape.

f Telescopes magnify distant objects in the night sky. They use lenses and mirrors to make things appear closer and larger.

Punctuation

a The earth is the third planet from the Sun (146 million kilometres away).

b Venus (named after the Roman goddess of love) is Earth's closest neighbour.

c Venus is also the closest in size to Earth (only 652 kilometres less in diameter).

d Venus spins from west to east (opposite to Earth).

e Venus is the hottest planet in the solar system (around 465 degrees Celsius).

Can you help?

People used to think comets were fireballs but that is not correct. They are actually frozen, lifeless bodies most of the time. They have solid centres of dirty ice surrounded by gas. They only come to life when they come near the Sun, because the Sun heats them up and releases gases trapped inside. These gases are what forms the tails of comets. The tails of comets can be millions of kilometres long—it is really only because of their tails that we see comets at all. Comets orbit the Sun just like planets but their orbits are far greater and so they last much longer. Some take thousands of years to complete their orbit. The most famous comet is Halley's comet, which comes round about every 76 years. The last time was in 1986, and it is expected to return in 2061.

Puzzle time

1 **a** Mars; **b** comet; **c** astronaut; **d** Jupiter; **e** meteorite; **f** Venus; **g** Saturn; **h** Uranus; **i** Neptune; **j** Mercury; **k** Earth; **l** galaxy; **m** Pluto

2 universe

3 astronomers

Chapter 7 Pages 50–57

What did you read?

1 The soldier is drinking and then sleeping; the boy is fishing.

2 Convicts and soldiers. The convicts are walking off the ship, and the soldiers are keeping them moving and in line.

3 **a** He is writing and that would be unusual to many of the people in the scene—that is, they may not be able to read or write themselves.

b The convicts would have been below deck on their long voyage.

c The Equator. Crossing the Equator was a very important event and the convicts were probably allowed on deck. This would have been the last time they had seen the sky.

d They have been on the ship for a very long time—about six months—and their legs are more used to a moving surface than to the stable ground.

e He is free and the convict boy is not.

4 **a** paragraph 2; **b** paragraph 1

How was it written?

1 interesting, three

2 **a** strangely quiet; **b** stamp up and down … shouting at the convicts … their tone is rough and angry

3 **a** flopped, squirming, gasping; **b** stagger, stumble, clutching; **c** stamp, shouting, pushing; **d** thrusts, twists

Spelling and meaning

1 **a** wretches; **b** thrusts; **c** gesture; **d** pitiful; **e** wanders, clutching; **f** stagger, stumble; **g** soldier, rough; **h** Although, wrapped; **i** swig, promptly

2 **a** shuffle, hobble; **b** flit, glide; **c** pace; **d** march, dash; **e** stamp, tramp, lumber; **f** glide, twist; **g** prowl, pace; **h** hobble, stagger; **i** totter; **j** scurry; **k** slither, glide

Grammar

1 **a** Their hair is knotted with dirt and straw.

b The trip across the oceans was harsh and long.

c Many of the women by the docks were carrying small children.
d Children played quite happily on the pebbly shore.
e I felt sick with grief and loneliness.
f Travellers led their weary horses to the water troughs outside the public house. (two phrases)

Punctuation

a The boys, hoping to reach the top by sundown, pushed on in the fading light.
b A small girl, hat tucked under her arm, smiled shyly at us.
c There are ten men in the room, all sitting around a small table, and they look up as we enter.
d My uncle, usually a rough-spoken man, gently asked the boy his name.
e The swimmers, exhausted by their adventure, flung themselves onto the riverbank.
f The students playing near the basketball courts are in trouble.
g The small children, kept awake by the noise, huddled together under the blankets.
h The old man, his eyes flashing angrily, refused to move.
i The boy looking this way is the thief.

Can you help?

I am sitting here in a café in the town square waiting for a parade to begin. Although the day is extremely cold, the crowd is huge. Everyone is very excited and very noisy as they wait for the parade to start. I can hear trumpets and drums. The parade has begun. Leading the parade are people on stilts wearing bright-coloured hats and flowing capes. One stumbles for a second before steadying up and continuing on. The crowd cheers. The stilt-walkers are followed by some very small children. Their faces are painted with animal masks and they are clutching balloons in their hands. Now I can see young girls in bodysuits doing cartwheels and tumbles. The scene changes every minute. Each time a new group appears, the crowd shouts out and cheers wildly. The biggest cheer is given to the town band at the end of the parade and to a little boy playing a very big drum.

Puzzle time

a baggage; b jetty; c porter; d deck;
e gangway; f passenger; g anchor;
h mast; i porthole; j captain

Chapter 8 Pages 58–65

What did you read?

1 She disagrees.
2 a people, animals;
b to give humans pleasure by showing them animals they would not otherwise see;
c education, conservation and research
3 b
4 Sumatran Orangutan/Black Rhinoceros

How was it written?

1 The introduction is quite clear but she changed it to make the start of her talk more interesting and to catch her listeners' attention.
2 a
3 Zoos and research 5, Purpose of zoos today 2, Zoos and education 3, Purpose of zoos in the past 1, Zoos and conservation 4
4 six times

Spelling and meaning

1 a cruel (this word can also be said with two syllables)
b survives, species, modern, believe, purpose, pleasure, research
c certainly, protection, endangered
d disappearing, conservation captivity
e international (five)
2 a century; b science; c excellent, exceptions; d Recently, celebrated
3 pleasure, satisfaction; vanish, disappear; aim, purpose; certainly, definitely; merciless, cruel; research, study; endangered, threatened; modern, recent; display, exhibition; benefit, advantage
4 a endangered; b research; c captivity; d species; e believe; f international

Grammar

a However; b for example; c As a result;
d Nevertheless; e Firstly, secondly

Punctuation

2 Possible answer:

In the past, zoos were exhibition parks. Their only purpose was to give humans pleasure, by showing them wonderful, exotic creatures that they would otherwise never see. Because animals were only there for the benefit of humans like you and me, no one took much care of them. They were transported thousands of miles around the world, then locked up in small, bare, lonely cages. In those days, zoos were cruel.

These days, things are very different. The whole purpose of zoos has changed. Now zoos have three major purposes: education, conservation and research. They aim to make animals better off everywhere. Because of this, the way animals are cared for is also different.

Can you help?

a/5 *They* buy them to look beautiful.

b/4 Of course, *the people* who buy animal furs and skins *nowadays* don't buy them to keep warm and dry.

c/1 Killing animals to make clothing is completely unnecessary *in this day and age*.

d/3 *They* did not have the technology we have *these days* to keep ourselves warm and dry using other materials like cotton and synthetics.

e/6 I wonder if *they* think about the poor animals killed in the process.

f/2 *In the Stone Age, humans* had to kill animals for their fur and skin, because that was the only way they could survive.

Puzzle time

R	B	P	E	Q	B	W	R	E	T	R	J	I	K	H	C	Z	I	O	P	L	F	S
F	W	U	R	H	A	B	I	T	A	T	T	V	H	G	F	E	Q	E	A	I	B	M
U	R	E	I	N	M	L	D	L	R	E	W	N	U	O	T	Y	B	V	E	H	Y	U
E	N	D	A	N	G	E	R	E	D	X	S	D	F	L	A	I	T	B	N	Y	I	L
I	L	B	P	S	R	P	O	P	U	L	A	T	I	O	N	R	T	Y	B	V	E	W
P	U	Y	G	S	Z	X	I	O	L	F	I	T	Y	U	R	E	S	E	A	R	C	H
P	R	C	M	O	A	L	B	C	E	W	R	F	F	A	S	L	R	B	F	E	O	U
A	O	X	N	G	R	P	R	O	T	E	C	T	E	D	U	T	R	A	T	H	W	R
R	Q	A	E	L	O	Q	E	N	T	Y	O	D	S	A	G	B	K	G	B	T	M	O
K	W	R	C	T	K	I	E	T	R	T	N	T	Y	N	I	A	Q	M	N	L	D	B
S	Y	T	R	H	L	Y	D	R	T	Y	S	P	E	C	I	E	S	T	R	S	E	T
Q	U	U	T	R	I	Z	I	O	R	E	E	T	Y	F	F	X	S	D	X	K	L	I
L	P	I	O	E	Y	N	N	L	R	F	R	D	G	H	J	T	L	J	H	A	P	K
O	K	P	G	A	Q	A	G	R	T	A	V	A	T	S	G	I	T	Y	U	B	V	F
R	S	O	F	T	W	F	M	E	G	P	A	R	F	H	U	N	T	I	N	G	K	J
T	A	A	S	U	D	D	G	W	Z	G	T	H	K	G	O	C	Q	W	E	T	H	F
B	E	C	D	Y	G	H	F	Q	F	O	I	T	J	F	I	T	A	L	H	P	R	O
V	F	O	Y	Q	M	T	S	P	S	G	O	E	Q	A	E	M	L	T	G	I	R	E
W	G	L	F	P	B	L	A	M	K	D	N	A	T	U	R	E	P	E	Q	T	U	A

Chapter 9 Pages 66–73

What did you read?

1 underwater earthquake, volcano, hurricanes, underwater landslides

2 **a** False; **b** True; **c** True

3 a break in the earth's crust

4 small earthquakes

5 a

How was it written?

1 Tsunamis are freakishly large waves which are usually formed when the seabed is disturbed by an underwater earthquake or by a volcano. / An earthquake is when there is a trembling or vibration (a 'quake') of the earth's surface.

2 **a** end of paragraph 1
b i end of paragraph 2; ii After second last sentence of paragraph 3

4 There is no right answer, but you might have said that diagrams would have helped. They usually do help the reader to understand explanations.

Spelling and meaning

1 catastrophic, caused, destructive, disturbed, earthquake, eruption, friction, hurricanes, landslides, livestock, occurs, shallower, tremors, vibration, volcano

2 **a** landslides; **b** caused; **c** disturbed;
d eruption; **e** tremors; **f** friction

3 **a** disastrous (disaster); **b** tragic (tragedy);
c destructive (destruction); **d** terrible (terror);
e horrific (horror); **f** shocking (shock);
g devastating (devastation);
h calamitous (calamity)

4 **a** origami; **b** kimono; **c** karate;
d karaoke

Grammar

b The tremors were felt by people living in tall buildings.

c Seismographs are used by scientists to measure vibrations.

d The main quake is sometimes followed by smaller aftershocks.

e Waves up to 10 metres high were triggered by two earthquakes on the seabed.

f The Richter Scale is used (by seismologists) to measure earthquakes.

g Earthquake 'hot spots' have been identified (by scientists).

Punctuation

At the back end of a glacier, high up in the mountains, is a large basin called the 'neve'. The neve is where the snow builds up and gets packed in ice. The long middle part of the glacier is called the 'trunk'. The ice from the neve slowly flows downhill and adds to the trunk of the glacier. Eventually, ice from the trunk arrives at the front end of the glacier—the 'terminal'. This is where the glacier melts, and comes out as a stream or river. As the glacier moves downhill it moves over humps and around bends in the valley. This causes the glacier ice to crack and buckle. The cracks formed are called 'crevasses'. When the glacier flows down a steep drop an icefall is formed. An icefall is like a waterfall but is made of glacier ice.

Can you help?

Glaciers are like huge rivers of ice that come sliding down from the mountains. High up in the alps, layers and layers of snow build up and get pressed together into ice. As the ice gets heavier and heavier, it starts to slide downhill. This moving ice is called a 'glacier'. Sometimes glaciers gradually expand and move forwards down the valleys into the sea, but at other times they gradually shrink and move backwards up into the mountains. When the front end of a glacier moves forwards, we say it is 'advancing', and when it moves backwards, we say it is 'retreating'.

Puzzle time

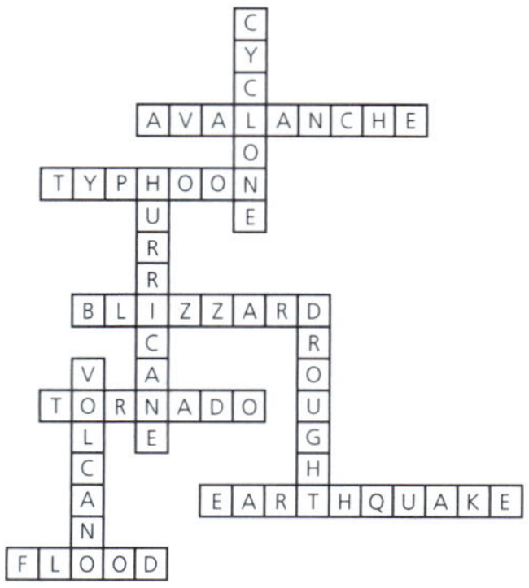

Chapter 10 Pages 74–80

What did you read?

1 a

2 a Children can aim for the same high moral standards.

b They fight for good no matter how hopeless things look.

c Any of these answers: Real-life superheroes are not particularly strong or brave. / Real-life heroes don't have special powers. / Real-life superheroes don't always win.

3 d

4 For

How was it written?

1 how long, names

2 to show that the writer has given equal thought to both sides and the discussion is balanced

3 a

4 another (para. 3), many other (para. 4), another thing (para. 6), also (para. 7)

5 You would probably tick all of these—all help to make the discussion quite clear.

Spelling and meaning

1 **a** whole; **b** benefits; **c** ridiculous; **d** drawbacks; **e** perfect; **f** qualities; **g** moral; **h** mutants; **i** particularly; **j** standards; **k** prejudice; **l** balance

2 **a** tomatoes; **b** potatoes; **c** volcanoes; **d** echoes; **e** mosquitoes; **f** torpedoes; **g** mangoes; **h** heroes

3

For	Against
Advantages	Disadvantages
Pluses	Minuses
Positives	Negatives
Benefits	Drawbacks
Affirmative case	Negative case

Grammar

a The Phantom is definitely the best superhero ever. 1

The Phantom is probably the best superhero ever. 2

The Phantom may be the best superhero ever. 3

b We should encourage children to watch films like *Spiderman*. 2
We must encourage children to watch films like *Spiderman*. 1
We could encourage children to watch films like *Spiderman*. 3

c Children could copy the behaviour of superheroes. 2
Children are sure to copy the behaviour of superheroes. 1
Children might possibly copy the behaviour of superheroes. 3

d Parents should always stop children watching these shows. 1
Parents should perhaps stop children watching these shows. 3
Parents should probably stop children watching these shows. 2

Punctuation

a Phantom's horse is called Hero.
b Superman's best friends were Lois Lane and Jimmy Olsen.
c It was the three villains' last attempt to get rid of Batman.
d Many children's television shows have no real heroes.
e Adults usually admire the superheroes' devotion to duty.
f The X-men's fight against evil never seems to end.
g The film's ending is a surprise.
h Fans can get more information about their superhero on the website.
i Batman's cave is beneath the city of Gotham City.
j Many different actors have played Superman.

Can you help?

Superheroes can be our guides in everyday life. Most people's lives, even children's lives, involve tough decisions. When faced with these decisions, we can ask ourselves, "What would Superman do?" I don't mean what special superpowers he would use, but what choices he would make in the same situation. Superheroes have to make some very difficult decisions in do-or-die life-or-death situations. Of course, their decisions might be more critical than the ones we have to make, but they can still teach us something about the responsible way to act.

Puzzle time

1

S	P	B	Z	R	P	H	A	N	T	O	M	P	M
U	R	O	B	I	N	J	V	U	L	T	U	R	E
P	A	F	A	K	R	Y	P	T	O	N	I	T	E
E	B	A	T	G	I	R	L	B	X	E	N	A	O
R	P	X	M	H	D	S	L	O	M	M	U	K	J
W	G	E	A	H	I	O	L	K	E	B	V	F	D
O	E	R	N	G	U	I	K	F	N	H	G	T	S
M	Q	W	P	G	O	T	H	A	M	C	I	T	Y
A	X	Z	B	S	U	P	E	R	M	A	N	L	K
N	G	H	J	S	P	I	D	E	R	M	A	N	H
W	O	L	V	E	R	I	N	E	W	V	B	A	M

2 man, spider, ram, mar, dam, pram, dram, mad, sad, sand, ride, side, spied, dire, sire, rise, near, dear, pear, pare, dare, mare, spare, spire, main, rain, drain, pain, sane, mane, pane, spear, pride, prime, prim, prise, dream, dries, drip (you might have found others)

Chapter 11 — Pages 81–89

Using your own words

1 Possible answers:

a Chinese New Year is one of the most elaborate, colourful and important of all Chinese festivals. Chinese people congratulate one another on getting through another year, and welcome in the New Year.

b In the traditional Chinese New Year, preparations started well beforehand. One day was set aside for the annual housecleaning or 'sweeping of the grounds'. After this, the family bid farewell to the Kitchen God or Zaowang. Everyone was very well behaved at this time because the Kitchen God would report on the family's behaviour. On the 23rd they farewelled the Kitchen God with a special dinner.

c One of the best parts of the new year was the Lantern Festival. Everyone carried lanterns into the streets and took part in a parade. The highlight of the parade was the dragon dance. The dragon was made of bamboo, silk and paper and could be 30 metres long.